A New Town's *Heritage*

Glenrothes 1948 - 1995

Keith Ferguson

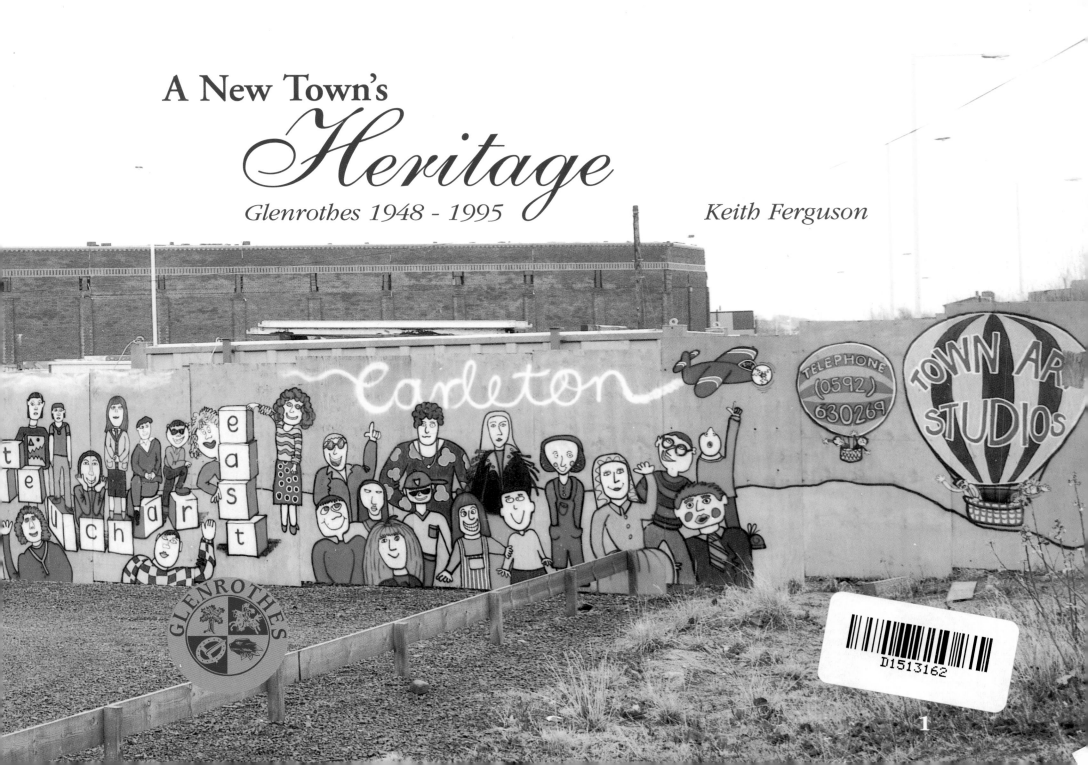

First published 1996 by Glenrothes Development Corporation.

Copyright 1996 by Keith Ferguson.

ISBN 0 9502603 4 7

Designed by Martin Bonnar
Produced and printed by AM Graphics, Glenrothes

Foreword

*I*n 1982 the Corporation published a History of Glenrothes by Keith Ferguson, then recently retired as its Director of Administration and Legal Services. That scholarly and exhaustive study was, and remains, the prime source-book for all those who would seek to know how a scatter of hamlets and farmtouns became the bustling and self-confident community which is Glenrothes.

In one sense the present volume brings that masterly work up to date. In another, probably more important, sense it calls time on the pioneering saga of economic and social assembly represented by the Development Corporation. As I write we are putting the final touches to our wind-up: our industrial and commercial assets sold to the private sector, our housing passed to Kirkcaldy District Council, our unique portfolio of skills and know-how dispersed. In too short an interval the final curtain will descend; indeed by the time this History appears it will all be over.

But the temptation to shed tears, and to complain about lost opportunities, should be resisted. Rather, there should be a sense of pride on the part of all those who have been concerned with this project. We who have to switch out the office lights inherited something special, and we take pride on behalf of all our predecessors in passing on now to other agencies the responsibility for maintaining the momentum. They will find it a rewarding task, Glenrothes must remain a pole for economic growth and regeneration in Fife. I am sure that Mr Ferguson's splendid postscriptum will help others to understand that essential truth.

Christopher Blake
Chairman

Introduction

Anyone who sets out to chronicle events has one great advantage. He or she can choose what to record and what to ignore, and colour that selection with his or her own views. This ability, however, brings with it a duty to select fairly and in an unbiased way. It is not easy. I apologise in advance therefore for the many omissions in the history which follows. Many events are unrecorded here, many worthy names absent, but a selection had to be made. I hope that what remains gives a balanced picture.

The years 1948 to 1995 are the years of Glenrothes Development Corporation, the years in which the task of creating a new town was undertaken and brought by them to fruition. Much of the history is seen through their eyes. This is only right, for they were always central to the creation of Glenrothes.

There was a choice between making this a full 'official' history or producing a largely pictorial record. In the event, I have tried to steer a course between the two. An outline of the official history had to be committed to paper, and it deserved to be illustrated.

It is to be hoped that the result gives a faithful account of the town's formative years, and will serve as one of the sources for other studies of that wonderful time. Much more is to be found in the Minutes and other papers of the Corporation and the local authorities, in the columns of the Glenrothes Bulletin and later the Glenrothes Gazette, and above all the memories of those who knew Glenrothes in the period 1948 to 1995.

My thanks are due to the Corporation who commissioned this book and made their records available to me, and to many others for their valued help, especially John Elder and my wife. Errors and matters of opinion are of course to be laid at my door.

K Ferguson

Keith Ferguson
January 1996

Contents - A New Town's Heritage

Glenrothes is born

Glenrothes was born on 30th June 1948 when the Development Corporation was set up under the New Towns Act. Its task was to "secure the layout and development" of a new town on 2,320 hectares of land stretching from the lower slopes of the East Lomond across the valley of the River Leven to just north of Thornton in Fife. On 31st December 1995 the period of fostered growth under the Corporation's guidance came to an end.

What led to the decision to create the new town? How did it grow over the next 47 years? And what legacy did the Corporation leave behind when it was finally dissolved in 1996? What follows is an attempt to answer these questions.

The Enabling Act

The idea of new towns dates from the nineteenth century with the publication in 1898 of Garden Cities of Tomorrow by Ebenezer Howard. They were designed to provide homes, work and recreation in balanced communities which would be the antithesis of soulless city sprawl. Letchworth and Welwyn Garden City were later created as a result of private enterprise, but neither Howard nor his successor, Sir Frederic Osborn, could persuade central government to adopt the idea officially.

During the Second World War this country had virtually two parallel Governments. While one was busy conducting the war, the other was planning for peace. In 1940 Lord Reith, the first Director-General of the BBC, was made Minister of Works, with special responsibility to prepare for post-war reconstruction. He appointed Professor Abercrombie to make a special study of Greater London. The latter's report envisaged a ring of satellite new towns around London to relieve pressure on that vast overcrowded city.

In 1945 a Socialist Government came to power, determined to forge a new Britain, and full of powerful personalities. Amongst these was Lewis (later Lord) Silkin, Minister of Town and Country Planning. Along with Reith and Abercrombie he persuaded the Government to accept the idea of publicly financed new towns. With minimum delay, the New Towns Act, masterminded by Reith, became law.

Coal - the gleam in the eye

The Labour Government of 1945 was committed to bringing about the regeneration of industry exhausted by the war. It also set out to ensure that power would not be lacking for that purpose, and in particular coal. A major step was the nationalisation of the coalfields.

Facing page: Mineral railway which served the mills, pre-designation

The doocot which was to give Dovecot its name

For many years the pits in Lanarkshire had been in decline, and new sources were sought in Fife, the Lothians and Clackmannan. Amongst these was Rothes near Thornton in Fife, where, as a result of an extensive programme of bores it was known that there were large reserves of coal. This was no new discovery. Coal had been mined in the area for centuries. The area of Rothes had been reserved in 1936 by Fife Coal Company[1] to provide road and rail connections. The first sod of Rothes Colliery was cut on 21st December 1946 by C Augustus Carlow, Chairman of the Company.

It was estimated that the workable coal within an area of about 10 square miles was about 120 million tons, to last a hundred years at a production rate of 500 tons a day. The Coal Board planned what was to be the most modern colliery of its day, using the "horizon" system of mining, with excellent facilities for the men, and railway marshalling yards said to be the largest in Europe.

Gestation

Planning for the post-war period was not confined to national level. In January 1944 Fife County Council set up an advisory committee to examine the county's resources and to make recommendations about its future development. The committee included representatives of industry, workers, agriculture and St Andrew's University, and appointed Sir Frank Mears as a consultant.

Over the next two years various public meetings were held, in which Augustus Carlow, a member of the committee, took a prominent part. While the idea of a Rothes Colliery with its employment prospects was well received, most people were opposed to the idea of a new town near Coaltown of Balgonie, though in favour of expansion of Markinch.

The view of the County Planning Officer, Maurice Taylor, was that a single new town would be faced with severe problems of co-operation with different local authorities, and that it would be preferable to have five or so townships of about 10,000 population near the coalfields.

The committee produced its report Fife Looks Ahead in 1946. This did not deal specifically with the idea of a new town, but proposed that the Council should as soon as possible "provide the housing and other amenities required for the development of the mining industry"; a County Housing Association should co-ordinate the efforts of the many housing authorities.

Cottages, Woodside from pre-designation days

9

What was once the main road to Cupar, now Alburne Park

However, other forces were at work. A draft New Towns Bill was published in April 1946. The Scottish Office stated that emphasis would first be on development of the coalfields in the east of Scotland, and that various suggestions were being considered for new towns in those areas[2].

In July 1946 Fife County Planning Committee had before it the draft final report by Sir Frank Mears to the Central and South-East Scotland Planning Advisory Committee. It was noted that for the Leslie/Markinch area 'a population of between 30,000 and 35,000 is expected to build up here, and a site is selected between Markinch and Leslie as the seat for a "constellation" '.

On 30th August a sub-committee met Mr Joe Westwood, MP for Kirkcaldy Burghs, and Secretary of State for Scotland. He put forward the Mears proposal for a new town in the Leslie/Markinch area with an eventual population of 30,000 to 35,000, needing 1500 acres. In later discussion, the County Planning Committee favoured an alternative site of about 2000 acres centred on Markinch.

A new plan produced by the Department of Health was put before the committee on 21st October 1946. This gave a sketch outline of a new town in what was called the "Loop Site" between Markinch and Leslie. There would be three neighbourhoods, two within the loop formed by the Markinch-Leslie branch railway line, and a third north of the Cadham to Leslie Road. Mr J H McGuinness, who with F J Connell was responsible for the project in the Department of Health, warned that even this site might be too small, and rejected the Council's Markinch proposal. With minor amendment the committee approved the "Loop Site".

More meetings followed throughout 1947, with Leslie, Markinch and Coaltown declining the chance of being part of the new town. Many names were suggested for the new town[3], but at the planning committee meeting on 4th July the choice came down to two, "Westwood" or "Glenrothes". By a narrow margin, it was agreed to recommend 'Glenrothes' to the Secretary of State. As "father" of the new town, Joe Westwood, who had tragically been killed in a road accident, would dearly have liked his name to be perpetuated[4]. The name "Glenrothes" commemorated the Leslies of Rothes who had owned much of the area, with the prefix "Glen" to avoid confusion with Rothes in Morayshire.

Representatives of all the interested authorities met Westwood's successor,

The 'towers' under construction at Rothes Colliery

Arthur Woodburn, on 12th December 1947. He blithely told them that he had decided on the name "Balgonie" for the new town. On being informed that this would be confused with Coaltown and Milton of Balgonie, he agreed to think again and to bear in mind the County Council's recommendation of "Glenrothes".

Shortly afterwards, Mr Woodburn decided again to enlarge the area to be designated for the new town, and also to accept the Council's choice of name. The Council continued to have reservations about the proposed area, but, having been assured that their representations would be considered, the planning committee decided on the casting vote of the Chairman, John Sneddon, not to take part in the coming public inquiry. It would have been an unfortunate start for Glenrothes if they had appeared as objectors.

In January 1948 the Secretary of State published the draft New Town (Glenrothes) Designation Order. In a memorandum[5], he described the need for expansion of coal production and for a new town to house a proportion of the extra miners; the basis for selection of the site; communications and services; existing industry and the effect on agriculture. Glenrothes would house 3,500 miners plus balancing population i.e. a town of 30,500 (later rounded up to 32,000). Ironically, there was promised a new road link-up to provide direct access to the south and replace "the present slow route via Kirkcaldy", a promise to be vainly quoted for a further 40 years.

A Public Inquiry was held in Kirkcaldy in March 1948 under the chairmanship of Mr J R Philip KC[6]. Objectors were the Thornton branch of the National Farmers' Union, Tullis Russell & Co Ltd, Fife Paper Mills Ltd and Sir Robert Spencer-Nairn. The Farmers' Union and Sir Robert objected to agricultural land being taken out of production. The paper firms feared the effect on the mineral railway, their future expansion, and the water supply from the River Leven.

The objections were repelled[7]. On 30th June 1948 the Secretary of State "in pursuance of the powers conferred on him by ... the New Towns Act 1946, made ... an Order designating as the site of a proposed new town an area of land extending to 5,730 acres or thereby in the Parishes of Markinch, Leslie and Kinglassie and the County of Fife ..."[8]

Glenrothes was born.

Preston School which served the area, pre-designation

Flashback

Most new towns were centred on sizeable existing communities, with their own histories. Glenrothes was placed in what was virtually a greenfield site, but that is not to say that the area was a historical vacuum before the new town was designated. There are strong traces of occupation in pre-historical times and many connections with Scotland's more recent past[1]. Every town deserves to know something of its "genealogy" and what follows is the merest summary as far as Glenrothes is concerned.

Pre-history

In December 1990 Glenrothes was host to the Third International Conference on Archaeoastronomy, a prestigious event in its own field. What drew them to the new town was the presence of the Balfarg Henge.

The existence of the henge was first suspected in 1949 when wartime aerial photographs were being examined, on which was visible the outline of a large circular ditch with a bank round it and a single opening. Despite the depredations of the plough, excavations which started in 1975 proved the existence of a large henge.

Henge monuments are unique to Britain. The Balfarg example consisted of an enclosure of about 4000 sq m within a ditch 5m wide and 2.5m deep. Inside stood a timber circle concentric with the ditch and probably two stone circles. The remains of the timber circle were well preserved. There had been sixteen upright posts, with deep sockets around which grooved ware sherds had been used as packing. Two outlying postholes showed the presence of a "porch" on the south-west side. Carbon dating indicated that the monument dated from about 3000 BC. From its size, it seems likely to have served a sizeable population for religious or ceremonial purposes[2].

In 1984 development of housing in the area was deferred to allow another full season's digging. The Balfarg housing site was planned around the site so as to preserve it.

1,000 years later than Balfarg, our forebears built the Balbirnie Stone Circle. This had long been known as the "Druids' Circle" and had been disturbed several times before professional excavation in 1970-71. Burial remains from different periods were found. Since the site lay on the line of future road widening of the A92 the stones were removed a short distance to a location near Balbirnie North Lodge.

Facing page: Traces of Balfarg Henge against its modern setting

Balbirnie Stone Circle

More Recent History

Later history of the area includes a tradition of the Danes establishing a fort on Goatmilk Hill at the site of the first golf course. The area was criss-crossed in medieval times by the tracks made by long distance travellers. One of these lay on Lady's Walk, the line of an old hedge in Woodside Road, and finally (the Tanshall and Auchmuty sections swallowed up by development) the old right-of-way between Newcastle precinct and the golf course there. In 1296 Edward I with his army paused in Markinch on his way from St Andrews to Stirling and must have passed through "Glenrothes". Rob Roy paid a visit in 1715[3].

The Balfour Family

Up to very recent times the area was dominated by two families, the Leslies of Rothes and the Balfours of Balbirnie. Between them the two families and their offshoots owned most of the land which was to become the new town[4].

The first mention of the name Balbirnie in relation to Balfours is in 1312 when "John de Balbrennie" was charged by Robert the Bruce with the defence of Dundee against the English. The estate itself was bought by George Balfour of Lalethan in 1650. His descendants were to distinguish themselves in public life, and in the development of agriculture and coal-mining.

The original part of Balbirnie House probably dates back to the 17th century. John Balfour is said to have started a series of extensions in 1777, for which John Nisbet, who had been associated with the Adam brothers, was responsible. General Balfour undertook a complete rebuilding of the house between 1815 and 1826, and the house as we know it dates from his time.

Robert Robinson of Edinburgh designed the landscape in the Capability Brown tradition. The Statistical Account of 1794[5] described the park as "delightfully romantic". Later work by Thomas White, landscape architect, led the 1845[6] Account to say - "These heights clothed with some of the finest trees in the country are rendered accessible on all sides by means of walks and alleys so contrived as to command at every turn varied and picturesque views of the surrounding country".

The Leslies of Rothes and Others

The ancestor of the Leslies, Bartolf, is said to have come to Scotland in 1057 with Margaret who was to become the saintly Queen of Malcolm Canmore. In the late 12th century his descendant was granted lands in Aberdeenshire and also acquired lands near Rothes in Morayshire. In the late 14th century Sir George Leslie came into possession of the lands of "Fythkill" (Fettykill), which later became "the barony of Leslie". George's grandson was created Earl of Rothes in 1457. In the centuries which followed the family was prominent in affairs of state in Scotland, none more than John the fifth Earl who became Lord High Chancellor in 1667 and was raised to the title of Duke in 1680; he died the following year with no male issue and the title reverted to an earldom[7].

The "Villa de Rothes", Leslie House, was greatly extended or improved by the Duke with the help of Sir William Bruce, architect and pioneer of the Scottish Renaissance. In its heyday it rivalled Holyrood Palace for size and grandeur, but three of its four sides were destroyed by fire in 1763. Eventually the cost of its upkeep brought about the downfall of the family. The remaining wing now serves as a Church of Scotland home.

In 1987 the original terraced gardens, built from the rubble of the fire, were restored by a community programme team. A flat area was the site of a large water garden in the Italian style mentioned by Daniel Defoe in his diaries.

The Stob Cross at Balbirnie East Lodge

Balbirnie House, once home of the Balfours

In 1966 an old building near Leslie House was being converted into an engineering laboratory when a marvellous collection of estate papers fell through the ceiling. These are a mine of information about the day-to-day running of the estate and house, as well as giving details of the Duke's extravagant funeral[8].

In 1677, the Earl, as he then was, imported one Thomas Alburne from England - "the best plasterer there ever was in Scotland". He was given land at "Wandersknowes", later to become "Alburne Knowe". Alburne Park was once the line of the A92, linking Edinburgh and Aberdeen by way of Pettycur, Cupar, and Dundee; this was a coaching route and opposite Alburne Knowe stood the "Plasterer's Inn", a staging post, on the site of the house "Levenbank".

Part of the designated area was also owned by Balgonie Estates. In 1635 the Castle and lands were bought by Sir Alexander Leslie, of a cadet branch of the Rothes family, Field Marshal to Gustavus Adolphus of Sweden, and General of the Covenanting armies. Another family name to appear in history was that of Archibald Pitcairn, Jacobite physician, the remains of whose house were restored in 1980; a relative gave his name to Pitcairn Island.

What was to become Auchmuty Farm was at one time a separate estate, but in 1670 the laird made a discreet getaway from his creditors and the estate was merged into that of Rothes. One of the Duke's subsidiary titles was "Lord Auchmoutie and Caskieberrie".

The Rothes estate was finally sold off in 1919, but its name survives in the name of the new town, and its farms gave names to most of the precincts.

Agriculture

Agriculture was of course the staple industry in the area from time immemorial, and no doubt provided considerable employment. Until comparatively recent times the "touns" housed all the craftsmen who supported farming. There was little sale of produce from the Rothes farms, but, with their own limeworks at Balgeddie and Stenton, the estate was largely self-sufficient.

While the local soil was not naturally productive, it had gradually been brought to a standard which merited high classification in the eyes of the Department of Agriculture, giving grounds for objection at the time of designation of Glenrothes. For the first 20 years or so clearance had to be

Leslie House, once home of the Earls of Rothes

19

Tullis Russell mill, major employer pre-designation and still in 1995

got from the Department for each new development.

Mining

Coalmining in Fife is recorded from the 13th century and was always the preserve of the landowners, who might however lease it out. A Feu Charter of 1555 of land at "Stentoun" granted licence to the tenants to dig for coal at their own expense, paying to the convent every ninth load.

The Leslies and Balfours engaged in the industry. Mining took place at Cadham before 1730, though the seams there could not be worked properly without co-operation from the Balfours - and they were rivals! Work continued until the late 19th century. Cadham indeed was originally a colliery village.

The Rothes papers have much detailed information about the workings and the wages and conditions of the colliers, not only at Cadham but also at Easter Strathore - not far from the site of the 20th century Rothes colliery. Though trial sinks in 1727 showed a large field of coal, water even then was seen as the problem.

In Balbirnie estate a "sill" of coal ran along the River Leven between the sites of Balbirnie Mill and Auchmuty Mill. Coal was worked initially from the riverbank, and later by shafts scattered over the estate, one very near Balbirnie House itself. Work went on till about 1880.

The result of all this was that in the 1970s throughout Cadham and Balbirnie a great deal of money had to be spent on "capping" old shafts and otherwise making old workings safe before development could take place.

The Mills

The banks of the River Leven near Leslie and Markinch had always been host to industries using water power. The River Leven Act of 1827, and the consequent partial drainage of Loch Leven and channelling of the river, brought control of the flow of water and so an upsurge in such industry.

No doubt the cottagers in the area benefitted from the growth in textile employment, but the main effect was the encouragement of the papermaking industry which was thriving at the time of designation and still continues as a major employer in the new town.

Thus Tullis Russell & Co is still the largest privately owned paper manufacturer in Europe. Originally it consisted of two mills, the Rothes (1806) and Auchmuty (1809). The Tullis family joined in 1836 and the Russell family in 1874, the name Tullis Russell & Co appearing in 1906[9].

A former manager established his own business in Balbirnie Mill in 1816. This became Fife Paper Mills, which after a whole series of new names, has become Sappi Graphics today. A former partner went off in 1859 to help found Smith Anderson & Co in nearby Leslie[10].

Thus, though there was no Glenrothes before 1948, the area brought to the town its own historical and industrial heritage.

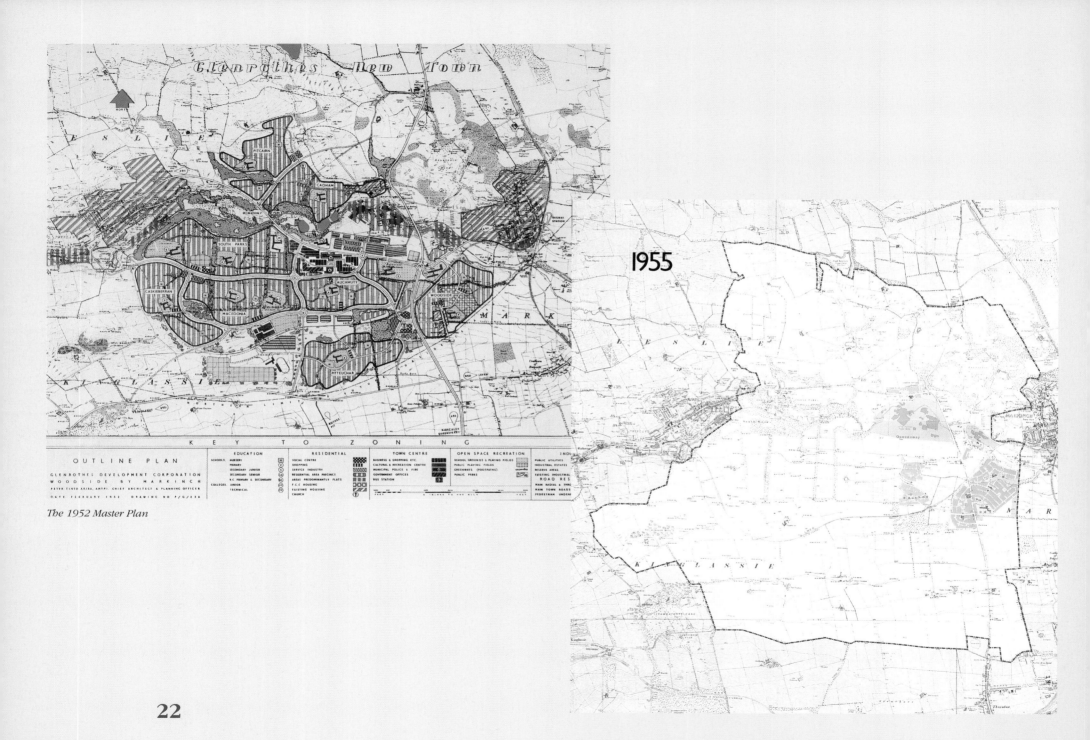

Glenrothes New Town

1955

KEY TO ZONING

OUTLINE PLAN

GLENROTHES DEVELOPMENT CORPORATION
WOODSIDE BY MARKINCH
PETER TINTO ARISA, AMTPI, CHIEF ARCHITECT & PLANNING OFFICER
DATE FEBRUARY 1952   DRAWING NO P/G/23A

EDUCATION
SCHOOLS. NURSERY
PRIMARY
SECONDARY JUNIOR
SECONDARY SENIOR
N.C. PRIMARY & SECONDARY
COLLEGES. JUNIOR
TECHNICAL

RESIDENTIAL
SOCIAL CENTRE
SHOPPING
SERVICE INDUSTRY
RESIDENTIAL AREA PRECINCT
AREAS PREDOMINANTLY FLATS
F.C.C HOUSING
EXISTING HOUSING
CHURCH

TOWN CENTRE
BUSINESS & SHOPPING ETC.
CULTURAL & RECREATION CENTRE
MUNICIPAL POLICE & FIRE
GOVERNMENT OFFICES
BUS STATION

OPEN SPACE RECREATION
SCHOOL GROUNDS & PLAYING FIELDS
PUBLIC PLAYING FIELDS
GREENWAYS (FOOTPATHS)
PUBLIC PARKS

INDU
PUBLIC UTILITIES
INDUSTRIAL ESTATES
RESERVE AREAS
EXISTING INDUSTRIAL
ROAD RES
MAIN RADIAL & THRO
MAIN TOWN ROADS
PEDESTRIAN UNDER

The 1952 Master Plan

22

Child of the Pit

Government had recognised from the start that local authorities could not effectively create new towns, bearing in mind their existing burdens of administering local services, developing and redeveloping. The first task of the Secretary of State on designating the site of Glenrothes was to appoint a Development Corporation. Over the years this was to consist normally of eight members[1], including a Chairman and Deputy Chairman, all part-time and paid. Usually the membership was to consist of roughly half who were members of the local authorities, and half who came from further afield but who brought with them particular expertise of industry or commerce.

The Corporation was a "body corporate" and took its powers from the New Towns Acts. These powers were fairly extensive and there were few things that a Corporation could not do, always assuming that it had the Secretary of State's permission. He gave general directions as to how it should operate, and his specific approval was necessary for all projects over a certain value. The Corporation was obliged to borrow money from the Treasury to finance its undertakings; the fact that the latter would allow borrowing only over a long period (usually 60 years) proved to be an irksome and costly restraint[2].

It was the Corporation's statutory duty to secure the proper layout and development of the new town in such a way as might be approved by the Secretary of State. From time to time therefore the Corporation had to submit proposals to him showing how it was intended to develop certain areas. The proposals dealt not only with the planning, but gave estimated costs of development and projected returns. Arrangements had to be made for the necessary supporting services to be provided by the relevant local authorities, and, wherever possible, to encourage private commercial interests to invest money in the town.

The first Chairman was Sir Hector McNeill, former Lord Provost of Glasgow, who died in October 1952 after making a great impression in the town's early years. The Deputy Chairman was Mr John Sneddon, a prominent member of Fife County Council and later its Convener. Along with George Sharp he had been much involved in discussions prior to designation. (It became general practice throughout the Corporation's life to have the County/Regional Convener as Deputy.) Other members were Lady Ruth Balfour, Major R L Christie, Dr L T M Gray from Edinburgh, Mr J M Mitchell then County Clerk of Fife, Bailie David Wright of Kirkcaldy, and Mr James Wright CA from Carnoustie.

Chapter **III**

Corporation members and officials unfurl the flag at the site of Woodside offices

The Corporation's first formal meeting was in St Andrew's House, Edinburgh, on Friday 5th November 1948, marked by a preliminary address from the Secretary of State.

Over the next 47 years Glenrothes was to have many ups and downs. The period can now be seen as having three distinct phases. From 1948 to 1962 the town was to grow in fits and starts, its star linked to the fortunes of Rothes Colliery. During the years 1962 to about 1982 the town took its place as an industrial growth point and developed its ultimate shape. The final phase, 1982 to 1995, was the time of consolidation, of attracting essential features previously missing, of preparing for dissolution[3].

Settling In

One of the Corporation's first jobs was to find a home for itself. In this (despite having been objectors) Tullis Russell were very helpful. The first meeting held actually in Glenrothes was in Auchmuty House on 20th July 1949.

After an abortive application in respect of land further south, planning permission was received for offices at the southern entry to Woodside village.

The new offices, which were to be the Corporation's home for the next 14 years, sometimes known as "the hutted encampment", were completed on 5th July 1950 at less than the estimated cost of £18,000, and opened by the Secretary of State on 6th September. Veteran staff will tell you that these were better for inter-departmental co-operation than any later homes.

The first General Manager was Frank Preston, Burgh Surveyor of Milngavie, who had made his name in the Scottish Council (Development & Industry) and Scottish National Housing & Town Planning Council. The first Chief Architect & Planning Officer was E A Ferriby, soon however to be succeeded by Peter Tinto. Jim Roger, the assistant to the County Clerk most involved in pre-designation work on Glenrothes, became the first Secretary & Legal Adviser, Jim Young became Finance Officer and Harold Pollitt Chief Estates Officer, a job which then included housing.

Planning

Apart from the hamlets of Woodside and Cadham the designated area contained only a few scattered farmhouses and cottages; the total population was around 1,000. The planners thus had virtually an empty canvas on which to draw.

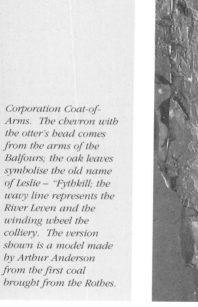

Corporation Coat-of-Arms. The chevron with the otter's head comes from the arms of the Balfours; the oak leaves symbolise the old name of Leslie – "Fythkill; the wavy line represents the River Leven and the winding wheel the colliery. The version shown is a model made by Arthur Anderson from the first coal brought from the Rothes.

Much preliminary planning had been done in the Department of Health, and there were few changes in the Outline Plan which was submitted to the Department and published in 1951. This accommodated a population of 30,000 to 32,000 people, a target based on the number of miners expected to be housed and a ratio of 1 to 8 or 9 of other people. So that there would be other employment for the wives and children of miners, there would be two small industrial estates, Queensway and Warout.

Under these proposals only about 2,000 of the available 5,730 acres were to be developed. Development would first be in the east-west valley of the River Leven down to the Warout ridge, where services were easiest to instal. The area north of the river, up to the lower slopes of the East Lomond, might, it was thought, never be needed. Development south of Warout ridge was to be limited by workings coming north from the colliery as far as a known geological fault.

The area was one of great natural beauty, especially in the landscaped policies of Balbirnie in the north-east and the remnants of the Rothes plantations in the west. The planners resolved to retain as much as possible in "green belt", and to emphasise the importance of landscaping.

The actual layout of the town was, in line with the thinking of the day, to be based on precincts of around 1,150 houses giving a population in each of 4,000 to 5,000. Such a population, it was thought, was enough to justify a corner shop, a church, and a community hall. For each neighbourhood of two or three precincts there would be a small shopping centre and a junior secondary school. Layouts were to be fairly traditional in the early years. Unfortunately, financial straitjackets meant narrower roads and fewer garages than the future deserved.

Early in the life of the town most of the land was bought. This was "juggled" over the years to keep farms going as viable units as long as possible, while at the same time allowing smooth sequence of development.

The Black Hand of Coal

What neither Fife County Council nor the Corporation could plan was the success of the Rothes Colliery on which the town's growth was dependent. During the early years many meetings were held at which council representatives expressed concern at the slowness of progress and the resultant lack of rateable return on their investment[4].

This concern was expressed at a meeting in St Andrew's House on 2nd August 1950. Even at that early stage the indication was that the eventual population could be less than the 32,000 planned for, and a maximum of 18,000 within the next 20-25 years was talked of. Nevertheless, the Corporation decided to press on with main services etc for the east-west belt south of the river, which could house 23,000. In November 1953 St Andrew's House directed that Cadham (neither acquired nor serviced) should be the next area to be developed, with no development west of Rimbleton.

In 1954 there were indications that a target of 15,000 to 18,000 might be too high. Then the NCB promised to speed up their development, with first production in 1956. All this made it impossible to plan smooth and rounded growth of the town. The Corporation, always in the dark about the pit's manpower needs, made some very undiplomatic comments to St Andrew's House about lack of support.

In November 1955 the Department announced that the Corporation should not enter into any further housing commitments until the manning of the Rothes Colliery had caught up with the town's progress, the present housing contracts being able to meet need until mid-1958. The arithmetic was dubious; official

Early Woodside – a supermarket giant in the making?

assurances that the original conception and purpose of Glenrothes were intact, and that they would continue to help to secure industry for the new town, were greeted with hollow laughter. The Government had neither sanctioned advance factory building, nor "planted" some Government agency in the town as they had done elsewhere. In 1956 a "Glenrothes Action Committee" put forward a document entitled "The Stated Case", setting out the arguments for continuing with the development of the town. The local Unions also made their feelings known.

It seemed that dawn was breaking in 1957. The furnishing of No. 1 Shaft at Rothes was completed and new "roadways" were being driven from No. 2 Shaft. The colliery officially came into production on 10th June 1957. Meantime, new marshalling yards at Thornton were finished, technically the most modern in Europe at the time.

It was a false dawn. In November 1959 the Secretary of State announced that, in view of a lessening in demand for coal, there would be a reduction in the numbers of incoming miners with their families. Glenrothes would have to turn more to Glasgow Overspill and other industrial development.

Demand for coal was not the only critical factor. Rothes Colliery was experiencing more and more difficulties because of geological faults and flooding, freely forecast by the old miners of the area. Eventually in 1961 it was decided to close the colliery down, and the central planning objective of the new town finally disappeared.

In a lively Adjournment debate in the House of Commons on 4th December, W W Hamilton MP, whose ability was often obscured by his views on Royalty, spoke of the loss of employment, the failure to make Glenrothes a "development district", and the lack of impact of Glasgow Overspill. The Government response referred to industrial development but did not promise "development district" status.

Housing

In the first phase of development, housing pursued an irregular graph. In the beginning progress was seen as urgent and for practical reasons was alongside the old A92, Woodside Way. The first developments in fact were under Fife County Council, 150 traditional and 158 "Stuart" houses.

By 1950 the Corporation's first contracts were under way in Woodside and Alburne Park, the latter mainly for staff initially. Lady McNeill, wife of the Chairman, officially opened the first house completed in Woodside 1st Development on 4th July 1951. Mr W S Gourdie was tenant of the first Corporation house to be allocated at 28 Woodburn Road.

The next precinct to be built was Auchmuty, which coincided with the intake of many of the miners from the west of Scotland destined for the Rothes. Between them, Woodside and Auchmuty formed much of the first phase of the town's development, from 1950 to 1960.

The earliest house designs, limited by controls on materials, were not greatly different from those of prewar. Layouts too echoed prewar "Garden City" ideas. Both designs and layouts would evolve gradually over the years, but not in any dramatic way. The architects wanted Glenrothes to be a "comfortable" town, not wildly experimental. Peter Tinto was determined, however, to introduce colour when possible, saying that the east coast climate was "sometimes grey"!

The pace of house-building grew from 20 in 1951 to an average of 320 over the period, well below what was expected of other new towns, but related of

*The first new employers at Glenrothes, the Scottish Milk Marketing Board –
the Creamery in production*

course to colliery needs. At this stage the population of the town was a youthful one, attracted by employment, but planning took account of future needs of the elderly. One group actually built for the latter and for disabled miners was "Coronation Cottages" in Woodside Road, later repeated in Auchmuty.

The first phase also saw the start of Rimbleton and South Parks precincts, largely completed by 1965. Here there were new designs, using culs-de-sac, pends and pedway routes. Greater variety of materials brought change and colour. South Parks 4th Development was built to slightly better standards, with a view to either sale or increased rentals; eventually it was to prove the highest sales area.

Industry

Industry, other than coal, was to help produce a balanced community in the new town. Unfortunately the task of attracting new industry was not made easier in the early years by the refusal of the Government to give Glenrothes "development district" status (which would have improved the terms available to incoming industry), or to sanction advance factory building.

Nevertheless, work went ahead on the layout of Queensway Estate and the first modest success was the creamery of the Scottish Milk Marketing Board in 1958. It was around the same time that Frank Preston, on a casual visit to the offices of the Scottish Council (Development & Industry)[5] in London, learned that Beckman Instruments Ltd were looking for a site and had met difficulties south of the border. The chief selling point of Glenrothes for electronics industries was the clean air, and after long negotiations Beckman's agreed to come. Their arrival in 1958 was a milestone; they attracted others; their manager Jack McNally was a great salesman for the town.

A year later Anderson Boyes & Co arrived to manufacture mining machinery. As well as retraining former miners, they brought with them a tradition of training engineering apprentices, a valuable asset. Though they survived the Rothes Colliery, and were to prosper for some years with sales further afield, they were destined eventually to succumb in the general decline of coalmining.

In 1960 another significant capture was Hughes Microelectronics, always in the forefront of the industry. They would develop eventually into the town's largest new employers. With Beckman and Hughes and other electronics industries which followed, Glenrothes was in the forefront of creating Scotland's "Silicon Glen".

Cessna were brought to a small unit in Queensway in 1961, and the Corporation at last got permission to embark on a programme of advance factory building. Yet the Corporation still had to compete on unequal terms with other development areas.

The Daily Shop

In the pioneering days the town was a mecca for travelling vans, supplemented by "Kate's Shop" on Woodside Way opposite the Woodside Inn, and Cruden's Chip Shop, a wooden hut at the top of Lady's Walk. The alternative was a trip to Markinch, or more rarely, to Kirkcaldy. Though often criticised, the vans performed a much needed service. Later, as new shops sprang up, they moved on to developing areas until these in their turn justified permanent facilities.

From these early days Markinch Co-operative Society pressed to be allowed to provide a service to the various parts of the town as it grew. Their faith in Glenrothes would of course culminate in their being the first department store

30 June 1958: HM The Queen signs the Visitors Book at Woodside Shopping Centre

in the town centre.

The first new shops appeared in Bighty in the summer of 1952, followed by the Otter's Head - the first Corporation-built public house, taking its name from the Coat-of-Arms. However, over the next few years planning was bedevilled by the uncertainties about the town's future.

In 1952 the Corporation invited tenders for the Woodside Shopping Centre and Community Hall. What now seems like overprovision for Woodside was in fact a desperate attempt to have at least a mini-town centre, should the town's growth be drastically cut. The project was completed in 1954 and in fact for the next 8 or 9 years acted as a town centre. It was here that presentations were made to the Queen on 30th June 1958, the town's 10th birthday.

Despite all the gloomy predictions about the future of Glenrothes, the foundation stone for the town centre was laid on 6th April 1955 by Sir Patrick Dollan, then Chairman of East Kilbride Corporation. At least, all Glenrothes knew it heralded the town centre; the Treasury's fall-back position was that the group of shops would be the neighbourhood centre for Auchmuty.

In the first Outline Plan there had been reserved some 63 acres at the town centre, to provide shops, hotels, cinemas, public buildings, offices and flats. At the time this must have seemed wildly optimistic; eventually it was to prove barely enough.

When the town began to develop westwards in the late 1950s, it was possible to make firmer plans for the town centre. A decision was taken that roads would serve only the perimeter and that the centre itself would be enclosed.

As an interim measure a group of shops was opened in South Street, beside St Columba's Church in 1960 to serve Rimbleton and South Parks. Later on they would be closed when Glenwood Centre was fully running[6].

Unfortunately the building of the first phase of the town centre proper suffered many setbacks for various reasons, but in 1961 the first contract was let[7]. This covered Albany Gate, what would become Lyon Square, and the Golden Acorn Hotel[8]. A tangible reminder of Sir Garnet Wilson's chairmanship of the Corporation is the clock which stands at the eastern entrance to the centre.

Beckman's factory begins to take shape

Carleton Primary School is officially opened

Educating the Infant

The only school at designation was the tiny Preston School, but Fife County Council very quickly started new buildings at Bighty Road and Carleton. The former was opened in 1951, first for primary children, and later - when Carleton was completed - nursery pupils.

Until 1957, when Auchmuty School was opened for secondary schooling, older pupils had to travel to Buckhaven, Cupar or Kirkcaldy. ("Highers" pupils continued to have to travel until 1966 when Glenrothes High opened.)

End of the First Phase

By 1962 therefore the town was poised for a change in direction. The pit was gone; there had been some industrial success; advance factories were on the way; the new A911 from the Beckman roundabout to Leslie was open; South Parks Road was being extended to Cabbagehall; layouts were being finalised for the West Neighbourhood. The Corporation had gained in 1961 a formidable new ally in the shape of Glenrothes District Council.

The Growing Laddie

Emerging in 1962 from the depression of the pit closure, Glenrothes had to give fresh thought to its objectives. Clearly the target population of 32,000, linked to incoming miners, was no longer relevant. During a visit to the town in March 1962, Lord Craigton, Minister of State, had emphasised a change to general industrial development.

Early in 1963 the Corporation, with the support of the District Council, submitted a memorandum to the Secretary of State proposing a revised population target of 55,000. Amongst other things, it was said, this would provide a greater pool of labour and enhance the town's attractiveness to industry; it would allow greater help for Glasgow Overspill; and it would justify more varied shopping, cultural and recreational facilities.

As it turned out, St Andrew's House was at the same time putting together a White Paper on the economic future and development of Central Scotland, basing its proposals on the idea of "growth points"[1]. The Glenrothes submission was therefore welcomed with open arms, and in October 1963 the Secretary of State announced a revised target of 55,000; the Corporation should allow for expansion eventually to 70,000, though there was no guarantee as to what agency would be responsible after 55,000.

Much later it was to be realised that this new target was not realistic in the Corporation's lifetime, but it was logical at the time. A figure of 55,000 was what the designated area could comfortably contain in light of house occupancy rates then existing. Also, it was widely held that an industrial town should have a population of between 50,000 and 70,000 to create a sufficient pool of workers.

Planning

One immediate result was that the Master Plan had to be revised. The land needed for housing, industry, town and neighbourhood centres, and recreation had to be re-assessed on the basis of the new target.

This brought a new difficulty, in that areas which might previously have escaped development were now brought into the frame. Of these Cadham, Pitcairn and Balbirnie, had much ground which was unsafe for building because of coal outcrops and old workings. Another factor in the northern area was the sloping nature of the land, unlike the comparatively flat central belt. This was both a problem and an opportunity for the planners to try new styles of layout.

At the Master Plan exhibition, September 1970

After much research a new Master Plan was produced in 1970. There was enthusiasm in the town. An exhibition of the Master Plan in the town centre was visited by no fewer than 10,566 persons, and in the evenings local clubs etc showed their hobbies and activities in the town centre.

Housing

The 1960s saw further advances to the west Macedonia and Tanshall being undertaken in 1964 to 1967. These precincts were the first to be laid out according to the "Raeburn" principle, ie with separation as far as possible of vehicle and pedestrian; the concept was to be modified in later precincts. Macedonia and, to a lesser extent, Tanshall were designed with flat roofs - fashionable at the time and not requiring clay roof tiles which were in short supply.

Pressure built up from the Government to speed up house-building and to take part in experiments in factory methods. Various ways were tried, including a small development by Hawthorn Leslie, the ship-builders, but the major effort was in the 12M Jesperson system. This was a product of John Laing Construction Ltd, who were encouraged to set up in Livingston[2]. A total of 482 houses in the form of 5-storey blocks appeared in Tanshall and

A new style of housing at Pitteuchar

Caskieberran. These were to need much refurbishment in later years. To some extent this was successful, for the first block was sold off in 1981.

Fortunately Glenrothes came late to high rise building. Though five blocks had originally been planned[3], the town's only venture into this type of building was Wimpey's Raeburn Heights in 1968. As a single block it was more successful than the ranks of tower blocks elsewhere.

Caskieberran and Newcastle precincts, built 1966 to 1969, were given new house types. An element of austerity was being introduced from now on; the influence was increasingly felt of SLASH (Scottish Local Authorities Housing Group), of which the Corporation was obliged to be a member, and which produced very basic designs and much standardisation of materials. Great ingenuity had to be used in layout and landscaping to make developments attractive.

Pitteuchar and Stenton followed from 1970 to 1977, after which the main thrust of development was at last to the north. House types in Cadham included a new feature of livingrooms being at first floor level. Early developments at Pitcoudie were an experiment by the Scottish Development Department in building contract and layout. Collydean brought the first experiment in pedestrian/car paths, the latest safety device.

The number of elderly in the town was growing. In April 1967 Fife County Council opened its Old Folks' Home in Napier Road. The first group of sheltered housing was opened by Willie Hamilton in 1979 in Jubilee Grove. In the early 1980s, the British Legion and Cheshire Homes appeared on the scene in Pitteuchar.

The 5000th house to be completed in Glenrothes was opened in February 1965 by Dr J Dickson Mabon, Under Secretary of State, the man at the heart of the drive for more houses; this was 21 Solway Place. The 10,000th house - 29 Hermitage Green, Stenton - was opened in September 1976 by Mr Gregor McKenzie, Minister of State.

For obvious reasons private housebuilding was slow to take off in Glenrothes. Apart from a small area in Alburne Park, the first breakthrough was Braid Drive in the 1960s. This was followed by areas in Newcastle, Pitteuchar and off Golf Course Road. The main location for such housing was to be in the northern and southern parts of the town. A start was made near Gilvenbank and in Whinnyknowe in the 1970s.

In earlier years building societies were not encouraged to lend on ex-Corporation houses, but from the mid-1960s sales began to pick up, so that by July 1976 there was a small ceremony to celebrate the 1000th sale of a Corporation house; by 1982 the total was well past the 2000 mark.

Industry

The fresh start given to the town in 1963 brought an upsurge in industrial enquiries.

Glenrothes was at last granted "development district" status, which was no longer dependent on high unemployment, and the Corporation was thus able to offer full financial incentives to newcomers. What the Government still did not provide was an East Fife Regional Road, but the advent of the Forth Road Bridge in 1964 and the Tay Road Bridge in 1966 helped to dispel the area's sense of isolation.

The town no longer suffered from the vagaries of the coal industry but the attraction of industry was subject to the stop-go economic policies of the 1960s

Early days in J B Butchart & Sons

39

and 1970s. Despite that, progress was steady. The older industries were active; Tullis Russell expanded in concert with an American firm. Though not directly connected, the first success for Viewfield Industrial Estate came in 1963 with the attraction of Sandusky from Ohio, making rollers for the papermaking industry. This was soon followed by Stowe-Woodward who put rubber coverings on old and new rollers.

Another notable capture in 1963 was J B Butchart & Sons, who, from making potato baskets in Perth, now expanded greatly into supermarket trolleys and baskets.

Many other successes followed over the period. The attraction of further well-known names in the electronics field raised the profile of Glenrothes to "Silicon Glen" level. Thus there were GEC-AEI (1965), General Instrument (1968), Brand Rex (1972), with supporting industries like Compugraphics (1970). The first two were later to leave the town, but offshoots remained.

Other new industries included Tokheim (1965), Thomas Salter (1965), Union Cold Storage and Velux (both 1972). Two of the most welcome features, however, were the way in which most firms expanded once they had settled, and the emergence of firms born of local enterprise like Fife Auto Cam & Tool, Forth Tool & Valve and McLean and Gibson.

Industrial Allies

In 1966 there was formed a Glenrothes Industrial Consultative Committee, which created a valuable forum for local managers to discuss matters of mutual interest, and often acted as a useful pressure group. In 1987 this was to grow into the Fife Industry Committee.

In 1968 the Corporation created a Dining Club to bring together academics and industrialists for informal meetings with the object of forming links between the two[4]. The Corporation acted as hosts. Initially only St Andrews and Heriot Watt Universities took part, but by the mid 1970s all 8 Scottish Universities were members, though Aberdeen later seceded temporarily. In 1975 Dr J W Midgely of Edinburgh suggested that the name be the "GUID" Club.[4]

The Corporation also took the initiative in the early 1970s in setting up a London Office, shared by the five Scottish new towns and available to local firms. This was seen as the forerunner of a "Scottish House", but the problems attendant on that are another story.

In 1982 came the formation of the Glenrothes Enterprise Trust, founded with help from local businesses, St Andrews University, Scottish Business in the Community, and the Scottish Development Agency. The Trust's purpose was to promote the establishment and well-being of small businesses.

Little Piggies

In all the foregoing account of industry 1962-82, mention has not been made of the infamous Cadco, but its influence cannot be ignored. Nor can the story.

On the principle that any publicity is good publicity it made the name of Glenrothes known; it was instrumental in the creation countrywide of a new checklist for new industry; it made available premises which might not otherwise have been approved.

The story started on 15 February 1963 when a retired insurance executive, David Black, appeared in Glenrothes as emissary for Cadco, accompanied by a Board of Trade official. After being thoroughly lectured on the advantages of Glenrothes, Black was sent on his way to see the Dundee authorities, the Corporation officials congratulating themselves that he was late and there was a blizzard.

The GUID Club in session

The first official plane to land at Glenrothes 6 August 1964, bringing Beckman Directors for a meeting (photograph by courtesy of The Herald and Evening Times, Glasgow)

Unfortunately, he was the innocent front man for Denis Edwards alias Loraine, a bogus ex-Squadron Leader, small part actor and producer, convicted confidence trickster, and owner of Royal Victoria Sausages of Hove. Behind Loraine were Tom Roe, a Solicitor and Tax Consultant in Geneva with a genuinely distinguished war record, and his client, George Sanders, the film star, a trained engineer, and author of "Diary of a Cad" which gave the name to the enterprise.

Soon the bait was taken. Cadco took over three advance factories in Queensway. After adaptation, these were to be used as a vast food-producing unit, based on the product of huge pig-rearing units to be built at Whitehill. A Phase II development would process vegetable and dairy products and make ice-cream, with also a packaging and printing block, film studio and a pie and bacon factory. Skilled and enthusiastic people were employed, and if certain problems, especially in the piggeries, could have been solved, the project could have come to some degree of fruition.

However, early on, Cadco complained that progress was too slow and insisted on using their own building company. This was fatal. Money paid out for building work done was not paid to sub-contractors but diverted to prop up

RVS. The sub-contractors were hardest hit in the inevitable collapse.

A Board of Trade Enquiry followed[5]. Loraine and Roe were later jailed for currency offences in Los Angeles and Switzerland respectively. Willie Hamilton complained that no criminal or other proceedings had been taken against anyone in this country[6].

Fortunately the factories were quickly made available for other industries; the piggeries, too, through the ingenuity of Chris Cramb, later a senior Corporation official, were converted into small workshops.

The Airfield

In its usual pioneering guise Glenrothes was the first new town in the UK to have its own airfield. This was opened to traffic on 6 August 1964 to great public acclaim, and became a centre for flying training and parachuting. The airfield was primarily intended as an aid to industry but apart from occasional use for board meetings etc that hope was not realised. In an attempt to improve its attractiveness, surfacing and realignment were completed in 1981 with European aid. The name "Fife Airport" was adopted.

The Daily Shop

It was always inevitable that commercial facilities would lag slightly behind population. Glenwood Centre, containing a hotel, 14 shops, the first purpose-built library, and a block of flats, came into operation over 1969 to 1971.

Glenwood was Corporation financed but the centre to serve Pitteuchar and Stenton - Glamis - was the work of MDW Developments Ltd. This was opened in 1975, comprising shops, bank, public house and library.

Most of the first phase of the town centre, including the Golden Acorn Hotel, was completed and occupied during 1963, and formally opened on 2 December 1964 by Sir Hugh Fraser. For several years the hotel became the hub of the town's social (and often official) life. Also at the end of 1964 Markinch Co-op opened their department store.

The second phase was the result of long consultation in the late 1960s, and involved the private sector in the shape of Neale House. (This was a partnership which was to endure right through to Phase IV). The glass roof was removed from the draughty square, which was refurbished and integrated into a large new mall. The "Kingdom Centre" as it was now called was opened on 1 July 1976 by Mrs R S Doyle.

In the late 1970s the partners decided to go ahead with a further extension. It had been realised from the early days that Glenrothes had to take into account the large and thriving commercial centre of Kirkcaldy. Now, in February 1979, planning permission was sought from Kirkcaldy DC who thought the proposals too large and too early. Fife County Council exercised its statutory right to "call in" the application. A Public Inquiry was held in September before Mr P Bonsell, with the District Council as objectors.

After a full hearing, the Reporter's recommendation in December[7] was to the effect that the proposed extension would not change the new town's place in the shopping hierarchy, and so was not in conflict with the Regional plan. Planning permission was duly granted and work started early in the new year. The third phase was trading by mid-1982.

Hospitals

For many years the age structure of Glenrothes was far below the Scottish average, many of the newcomers being young couples. The birthrate was therefore far higher than elsewhere. (One couple pressed for years to be

A trio of knights at the Town Centre opening 2 December 1964 – Sir Garnet Wilson, Sir John McWilliam, and Sir Hugh Fraser who performed the opening ceremony.

housed in the town believing that this would cure their childless state!)

Expectant mothers often had to make last-minute dashes to Craigtoun near St Andrews, a cause of regular unrest. In April 1965 Glenrothes mothers marched on the town centre calling for a maternity home in the town. A joint delegation from the authorities met Mr Teddy Taylor, Under Secretary of State, in February 1971, and pressed the case for hospital facilities, especially maternity.

The response was that a special maternity unit was to be provided in 1974 in Kirkcaldy where Glenrothes mothers would now go. A new hospital was however to be built in Glenrothes for geriatric cases and with day-bed facilities. The latter duly appeared and was opened in 1981.

Education

Over the period Fife County and then Fife Regional Councils continued their policy of providing primary schools early in the life of each precinct.

The big advance for the town was the opening in 1966 of the new Glenrothes High School. Early in the 1970s, with national changes in education policy,

Glenrothes hospital nearing completion

45

The 'new' Glenrothes High School

Auchmuty and Glenwood were also raised to "High School" status.

End of the Second Phase

In 1981 St Andrew's House stated that whatever the future outlook, new towns would have a major part to play as instruments for stimulating employment and underpinning the economy. Development Corporations would however remain only for so long as they were necessary to promote and achieve future industrial growth. Housebuilding must be undertaken increasingly by the private sector. When a new town was nearing its target population, the Secretary of State had in mind that its housing and industrial/commercial assets would be taken over respectively by the District Council and the Scottish Development Agency. In Glenrothes, and in the other Scottish new towns, a wind of change was blowing.

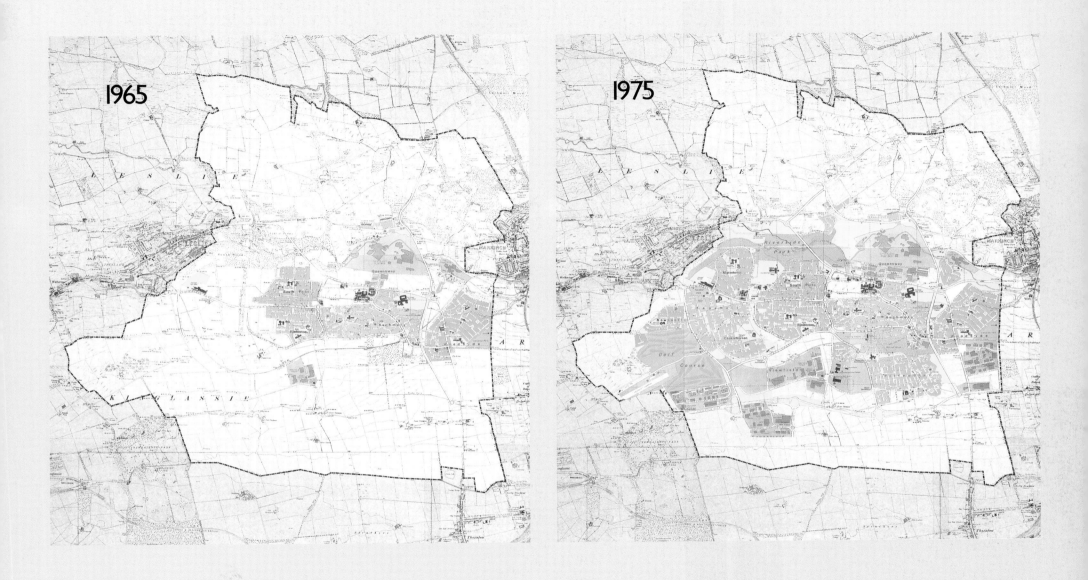

1965

1975

47

1985

1995

Preparing for Adulthood

*T*he Secretary of State's policy statement at the end of 1981 heralded the final period of fostered growth. Shortly after, he asked new towns to submit "Development Profiles". These would set out what remained to be done to enable each to become "an established mature community". This would allow them an opportunity to re-assess priorities and critically examine what each town had achieved.

The Glenrothes "Profile" was submitted in June 1983, setting out the remaining objectives. The official response was that progress towards winding-up the new town would be based on a "trigger point" of 79% of target population, ie 43,450, estimated to happen in the mid-1990s[1].

The final phase from 1982 onwards thus took place in the shadow of dissolution. It coincided also with a Government bent on diverting public expenditure into the private sector and the realisation of assets which it did not regard as the proper domain of the State.

Other factors affected planning and pace of growth. First, a severe economic climate slowed development for long periods and reduced levels of manning nearly everywhere. Secondly, the density of house occupation was much reduced, partly because of an ageing population, and partly because of changing social habits. This meant that the population grew very slowly but took up much more of the designated area than expected. At the same time private housing suffered periods of setback.

Shackles Again on Industrial Growth

At the end of 1984 the Secretary of State announced that Glenrothes was to be deprived of special development area status. Two results followed. There was a temporary upsurge in industrial building, some as part of the normal advance factory programme, but much through established firms hurrying to qualify for grants before they disappeared. Secondly, there was a noticeable falling off in interest and enquiries from prospective investors.

Glenrothes was left at a distinct disadvantage compared with other new towns. Meantime, Fife was experiencing rapid growth in unemployment, yet no part of the County qualified for special development status. Efforts to change Government policy were fruitless and the matter grumbled on for years.[2]

These efforts were not confined to haranguing government. It is impossible to list all the devices used to help to attract industry, but over the next few years,

Flight Simulator at Rediffusion Simulation Ltd (photograph by courtesy of the company)

apart from the normal promotional work, the Corporation expanded the GUID Club to the central colleges of Edinburgh; sponsored a Young Business Person of the Year Award with the Sunday Express; seconded staff to Locate in Scotland for the USA and Europe; sponsored the formation of a Fife Export Club; sponsored a trade seminar in Zürich; arranged a visit to USA parent companies in 1989; and so on.

Swings and Roundabouts

The 1980s brought a series of losses on the industrial front. In 1982 Burroughs closed[3]. Other casualties by 1986 included GEC, General Instrument; Thomas Salter, K & L Packers, Eurofasteners, and Haigs in nearby Markinch. Anderson (Boyes) Strathclyde closed in 1988[4].

The picture was not all gloom. Momentum was kept up through expansion of other firms such as BUKO, Beckman RIIC, Tokheim, Brand Rex with a new European HQ, and Velux with their HQ of revolutionary design. As the country began to teeter out of recession in the 1990s the conclusion was that, although some enterprises had been lost, Glenrothes, like the rest of Scotland, seemed to have ridden out the storm better than the rest of the UK[5].

Despite casualties, Glenrothes could still attract and keep electronics and other high technology developments. The town could fairly claim in the 1980s to be the hub of Scotland's "Silicon Glen".

1983 brought Applied Computer Techniques (Apricot) from Birmingham, later taken over by Mitsubishi. Former employees of Burroughs had a runaway if temporary success in Rodime. Soundtracs came in 1990. After agonising negotiations in Tokyo, Canon Inc of Japan, in the forefront of technology, announced that they would open their first UK manufacturing plant in Glenrothes in 1992; development was slow, but 1995 brought news of expansion in line with first indications. In 1994, a large unit was leased to Calluna Technology, a firm of great potential. Over the years, various Glenrothes firms won awards for export and innovation[6].

Union Cold Storage at Southfield closed in 1981 and for years the Corporation tried to bring this into multiple use. Eventually in 1989 it re-opened as the "Fife Food Centre", marketed as the only specific development in Scotland for the food industry with access to frozen-chilled and ambient storage, distribution and packaging. Advance units followed, taken by a variety of operators.

Canon comes to Glenrothes 1992

51

In 1994, a useful aid towards future expansions appeared, with the establishment of a Centre of Engineering Excellence by Oriel Training Services at Eastfield. A new Royal Mail road transport workshop opened nearby. Southfield saw the advent of Spraymasters, Micronas, and Climatic Services.

There was a flurry of activity in 1995. Birkby Plastics Ltd, suppliers to the electronics industry, agreed to set up in Westwood Park. Hughes Microelectronics broke all records. BICC Brand Rex got permission to adapt the former Crystals Arena[7] for expansion. BUKO, Velux, Tokheim, Rothes Data Services and BI Technologies (formerly Beckman Industrial) were all set to expand, the latter moving to refurbished premises at Eastfield[8]. Tullis Russell (now owned by its employees) decided to invest £2M in a primary treatment plant. Another pre-designation papermaker, Smith Anderson in Leslie, was pioneering in recycled products.

Said the "Scotsman" in August 1995, "Glenrothes remains the industrial nucleus of Fife, with an extensive stock of industrial properties and a diverse range of businesses from primary engineering to high-tech electronics".

Fife Airport

A determined effort was launched in April 1983 to derive more benefit from the airport. "The Glenrothes Challenge", aimed at aviation engineers and technologists, offered a top personal prize of £2000 for innovative thinking, and other incentives for those whose ideas might lead to new industrial or commercial enterprises on land adjacent[9].

Somehow, the airport and industrial park did not grow to potential. There were years of uncertainty about operators and lessees, but in 1995 the airport was sold to Tayside Aviation, operators at Dundee airport. An airport licence was issued by the CAA; a Fife Flying Club was formed; engineering maintenance was transferred; TA and University units expressed interest; training for Flying Scholarship candidates for the RAF started; terminal and restaurant facilities were to be completed. Perhaps the potential was at last to be realised.

Public Housing

Housing, in the final phase, went ahead on different lines, almost wholly to the north and south. In 1984 news came that the mainstream programme was to end; from then on new housing would be only for special needs. The

District Council was concerned about the implications for its own programme, and by the late 1980s there was a steady decrease in the number of family houses available for let.

In 1982 the Royal British Legion completed a sheltered housing project near Glamis Centre, and two years later Group Captain Leonard Cheshire opened Glamis House, a home for the disabled. From 1987 the Corporation's main effort was on houses for the elderly in Woodside, Stenton, Balfarg and Cadham, and the upgrading of cottages in Woodside and Auchmuty to sheltered housing. In a private venture in 1985 supported by Christian Alliance (Keychange), Gilven House became a refuge for homeless women. In 1986 single person flats in Pitteuchar and Stenton were started.

Limited developments for general needs were, however, later approved and undertaken in Balfarg (1988-90), Finglassie (1990), Collydean (1991-92) and Stenton (1993). In these, an eye had to be kept on demographic trends, for the average household size continued to fall far below that in the early years of the town's life.[10]

In line with Government policy to diversify tenure, the Corporation from 1990

Public housing in the 1990s, Collydean

sold all "new build" housing (apart from infill flats) to housing associations, thus keeping the houses available for renting.[11] By 1995 eight Associations were operating in the town, with over 800 houses between them, 14% of the total available for public sector renting.

House Refurbishment

The town was getting older. Some of the earlier houses and their surroundings had been showing the fact for some time, and a much greater effort had to be made from now on towards refurbishment. Schemes of improvement of houses and environment went on through the 1980s and 1990s in Woodside, Auchmuty and Macedonia. There were also special problems with Laing Maisonettes, Hawthorn Leslie houses, and some dwellings where asbestos had been used.

Anti-Social Tenants

Glenrothes was no better or worse than other towns as regards difficult tenants, but one case brought much media attention. A policy statement in 1993 said that the Corporation was "determined to do everything in its power to ensure that anti-social conduct will be thoroughly investigated and the Corporation will take legal action when evidence is obtained which will stand

Part of Balfarg Show Village, 1988

up in Court. This could lead to the eviction of anti-social tenants and their families". The message eventually bore fruit, evidence was obtained, and after a long Court battle the family concerned was evicted. Unhappily other cases remained.

Private and Other Housing

As forecast in 1981, even greater emphasis was placed by the Government on sale of Corporation houses and encouragement of private builders. The success of the sales effort may be judged by the fact that the 5000th sale was being celebrated in 1988, the 6000th in 1990, and the 7000th in 1994. By the time of disposal of housing stock to Kirkcaldy District Council in 1995 the total had grown to well over 60% of houses built over the town's lifetime.

There was steady disposal of land to private developers. An unusual venture was the Balfarg Show Village in 1989, 18 houses of different design showing the best of private housing available in Fife. Later, a self-build housing association got under way at Balfarg with a target of 27 houses. A nursing home also appeared in Balfarg.

For many years Glenrothes had been known as a "young" town. A sign of changing times came in 1995 when two planning applications were made for old folks' homes. This roused much controversy, one councillor alleging that the town was slowly becoming the "geriatric centre of Fife"! Also in 1995, local residents, the MP, and councillors took exception to a scheme by Collydean Community Venture Trust, chaired by Jack McNally, to build a 30-bed nursing home, medical centre, halfway house for teenagers, and a home for vulnerable youngsters, all at Pitcairn Avenue.

The Daily Shop

It was always difficult to strike a balance between town centre and neighbourhood centres as shoppers became mobile. Woodside and Glenwood suffered in the late 1970s. Cadham however welcomed the 1980s development of its neighbourhood centre, with public house, 10 shop units, offices, a public hall and library, and workshop units adjacent. In 1987 a refurbishment scheme for the Glenwood Centre was approved.

There was still a possible need in the outer precincts. A planning application was put forward in 1995 by a London company, Neighbourhood Centres (UK), for permission to build a group of five shops at Peploe Drive, Pitcairn, though local residents felt that fewer shops would suffice.

Part of the Kingdom Centre, 1984

The Town Centre

Phase III of the town centre opened in December 1982. At the end of 1983 the Golden Acorn was given a facelift by new owners, Stakis, and became the Albany. A notable newcomer was the entertainment centre of Kingsway Entertainments, including two cinemas which opened in October 1985.[12]

Phase IV, the final element of the Kingdom Centre germinated through the late 1980s. The need was seen to attract one of the big multiple retailers such as Marks & Spencer, while Lyon Square had to be kept attractive to shoppers, and the external aspect and car-parking had to be kept in mind. By December 1988 proposals were ready to be put to St Andrew's House, but the programme slipped badly as the various parties revised their sums.

Work finally started in October 1991, and in the later stages there was also thorough upgrading of the first and second phases. The first priority, however, was a multi-storey car park, with the promise by Fife Council of a later stack at the eastern end. The Council produced a much improved bus station and pedestrianised part of North Street. Most of the new shopping units were completed by 1994. So also were the magnificent Rothes Halls, built along with the fourth Phase, but more of them later.

By 1995, the town centre had been virtually completed. Some units had still to be let; some shopping gaps remained and there was still no national multiple; the "town hall" was in place; office blocks had appeared at regular intervals[13] and the Region now had a compact headquarters.

Saltire Park

In the 1980s it became clear that town centre space was limited, and that the town would have to look elsewhere for service and office employment. Viewfield North, later named Saltire Centre, Pentland Park, was developed for the purpose. Part of the Centre was sold to Caledon Park, who set about attracting retail warehousing. At the end of 1988 Texas Homecare opened, and in the following year, units were let to MFI, Carpet Care and English Rose Kitchens.

It took a long time to establish the principle that building advance offices was as valid as providing advance factories, but permission was given in 1989 for a 40,000 sq ft block at Saltire. The policy was emphatically endorsed when, in 1990, the Inland Revenue agreed to buy the building and took occupation in 1991. The Corporation immediately got permission to erect a sister complex, into which CSL Ltd and CFM Ltd moved in 1992.

A Corner of the Saltire Centre

How Do You Get Out of Here?

"Excellent road communications will also be provided by the proposed East Fife regional road which has been planned as one of the main approaches to the Queensferry passage". So said the Secretary of State in his Memorandum to the draft designation order in 1948. He and his successors "missed the boat" by a big margin.

The lack of the regional road for 40+ years was bad enough, but it was used to quash suggestions for other improvements. Whenever it was proposed that any of the accesses from the town to the M90 might be modestly improved, the response was not to be "parochial" and endanger the regional road; then the latter would again be deferred, an outcome which, one suspects, might have been "cooking" behind government curtains all the time.

However, at last the great day arrived with completion and opening on 16th July 1990 of the final phase of the East Fife Regional Road linking Glenrothes with the M90. The benefits do not need to be spelled out.

One longstanding bone of contention was the need for improvement of the Preston/Balfarg section of the A92. The dangerous junctions at Cadham and the need for dualling were repeatedly raised with the authorities. Though matters got to the stage of the design being ratified and shown to the public in 1990, the outlook was still bleak in 1995. The Government announced that there was no money to upgrade the A92; it would be 1997 at the earliest before the road was upgraded. Even that was conditional on money being available and no other trunk schemes being given higher priority.

Other main roads within the town did make progress. October 1987 saw acceptance of a tender for the remaining phases of the Northern Highway - Pitcairn Avenue. The town plan had also long shown a "western distributor road" linking the Leslie and Southfield roundabouts, and land had been reserved for the purpose. There was some criticism of the environmental effects[14] but traffic considerations prevailed. Nearing completion in 1995, the road again roused controversy when it was announced that the speed limit would be for the greater part 50mph.

The Secretary of State's 1948 Memorandum envisaged that "the internal road system ... could be so planned as to facilitate a frequent and rapid system of public transport ... to the station at Markinch". In the 1960s there was talk of a new halt near Coaltown of Balgonie, and in 1988 the authorities co-operated to provide new parking and a bus interchange facility at Markinch. In the same year Scotrail proposals for a Fife "loop" service raised the prospect of a new halt at Thornton. This was to be the first new station in Fife for 75 years, the cost shared by FRC, Scotrail, the European RDF, and the Corporation. The name "Glenrothes with Thornton" caused some anguish in Thornton with its long railway traditions.

Tourism

What at first seemed an unlikely course for the town started in 1985, with the attempt to create an image of Glenrothes as a base for holidaymakers. A Tourist Association was launched in 1986, taking its first steps towards becoming an independent organisation. Later, it became Fife and then Glenrothes Tourist Promotions Ltd, gradually increasing the range of promotional events, and working through the Information Kiosk in the Town Centre. Consultants were appointed in 1992; a scheme of improvement grants was devised for householders willing to provide B&B; a new Tourist Information Centre was opened.

It was perhaps a sign that Glenrothes was now firmly on the tourist map, when the "Brewers' Fayre", with motel, public house and restaurant, opened in 1995 at Bankhead.

End of the Corporation's Reign[15]

The "Development Profile" of 1982 set out what remained to be done to make Glenrothes "an established mature community". By December 1995, the objectives in the profile had been almost all achieved - main roads, drainage, rail halt, pedestrian bridges, parks, factories and industrial sites, offices, town centre and associated facilities, housing public and private. Only one major element was missing - improvement of the A92 between Preston and Balfarg. That was left in other hands

Other Legacies

*T*raditional towns grew up over hundreds of years. Each gradually accumulated its own distinctive heritage of church, landscape, parks, public and recreational buildings etc, through the efforts of authorities, individuals and benefactors. As far as possible, within the comparatively short life of the Corporation, Glenrothes had to be similarly "clothed" and "furnished".

Churches

In an era of declining adherence to the church, the efforts made by the various church authorities to provide for religious need in the town, and the contribution of the churches to its social life, were inestimable.

In the early years services were held in Carleton School and in the Mustard Seed Hall, Old Well Road. The foundation stone of the first church, St Margaret's, was laid on 29 September 1953, the opening taking place on 16 May 1954. In a town not known for architectural daring, some of the later churches were of radical design, notably St Paul's Catholic Church (1958), St Columba's (1961), and St Ninian's (1970). St Columba's was also given a novel internal design, said to be based on Reformation ideas, and enlivened by an Alberto Morrocco mural. In 1979 the congregations of the Baptist Church (1960) and St Luke's Episcopal Church (1962) found it convenient to exchange buildings.

Other denominations operating in the town were the Free Church of Scotland (in the Mustard Seed Hall), the Church of Christ, Jehovah's Witnesses, the Salvation Army, the Gospel Hall, and the Elim Pentecostal Church.

Landscaping

From the beginning it was realised that landscaping must keep pace with the building of the new town. The success of that policy was self-evident as the town matured, and it was achieved in many ways. From shrubberies and ground-moulding in housing areas, to woodlands and smaller groups of trees, from "Bodie's boulders"[1] to planting in roundabouts, every care was taken to bring life to the bricks and mortar.

When, in the 1970s, the nurseries near Leslie were being reduced, all the surplus stock of trees and shrubs was made available to the townspeople. National tree week in 1983 was recognised by the provision of 1000 trees for planting by local children. In 1995 the Scottish Woodland Trust took over the good work of woodland planting, together with the established woodlands[2].

Facing page: Interior of St Columba's Church with Alberto Morrocco's mural

Böblingen's gift to Glenrothes, 'The Defenceless One', with the tip of the new western freeway bridge peeping through the trees, 1995.

Much of the credit for the "greening of Glenrothes" in the second half of the town's life went to Landscape Architect, Kevin Brame, ably backed by John Coghill.

Sculpture and all that Jazz

The Corporation's first major venture into the art world was the commissioning of Mr Benno Schotz, the Queen's Sculptor-in-Ordinary in Scotland, to produce a centre-piece for the first phase of the town centre. The resultant work, entitled "Ex Terra", represents a mother and children growing in a tree-like form out of the ground. Three children can be clearly seen. Look closer and you will see six. The sculpture, later moved from Postgate to a site near the bus station, was unveiled on 19 April 1965 by Sir William McTaggart, President of the RSA.

Flushed with success, the Corporation commissioned a "water sculpture" for Lyon Square. This consisted of a fountain with water cascading down a series of coloured surfaces. Public reaction was less than adulatory and the feature was removed in 1969, never to reappear[3]. It was last seen in some workshop, waiting to be found and puzzled over by some far-off generation.

In one of those initiatives which came naturally to Glenrothes, it was decided in 1967 to appoint the first Town Artist. This was a revival of the practice in Renaissance Italy of including the artist in the building team. As a supplement to the work of the architect and planner, the artist's task was to give the town its own personality.

Thus, David Harding (1968-78), Malcolm Robertson (1978 until he was "privatised" in 1991), and many gifted assistants, gave the town a miscellany of features, such as heritage columns, a "henge", brick spiral and patterns; hippos, crocodiles, elephants, birds in flight, dinosaur; shoppers' group, seated figures, "Giant Hands", "Twa Heids"; a rainbow of underpass murals; mushroom, UFO, and so on.

For the town's 40th anniversary celebrations in 1988, an Edinburgh sculptor, Ronald Rae, was commissioned to produce "The Good Samaritan" for the town park from an eight ton block of white granite from Finland. In 1994 the Public Art Commission Agency borrowed the sculpture for an exhibition of Rae's work in Sheffield. It was returned in 1995.

As part of a refurbishment of Glenwood Centre, vandal proof security panels in a forest theme were erected. In 1990 these were commended by the Saltire Society.

The town's contribution to Glasgow Garden Festival in 1988, the Irises, later re-erected at Leslie roundabout, was given the John Brown Clydebank award for the "Most Original and Amusing Artefact" at the Festival.

In 1991, Malcolm Robertson's "The Dream" was presented to the twin town Böblingen as "Der Traum", modelled on local school children and symbolising children of the world playing together in friendship and mutual support. In 1991 a duplicate was unveiled in Glenrothes by Henry McLeish MP. Böblingen's present to Glenrothes was "The Defenceless One", now located close to the "Good Samaritan".

One of the most exciting ventures was the mural "Doing Things", on the hoardings round the Phase IV extension to the town centre. This roused great enthusiasm when it was broached in 1991, and 400 children participated in what became - at 686m - the longest mural in the UK.

Controversy was aroused in 1995 by a proposal to re-erect four cast iron

Potter at work in the Craft Centre, Balbirnie

columns from a London railway station. A critic described it as a "wind-up aberration"!

Balbirnie[4]

Balbirnie Estate was bought from the Balfour family in 1969. Traditionally, at the family's invitation, the people of Markinch had always walked freely in the grounds. It had all the ingredients of an outstanding park, with landscapes dominated by beech, but including other rarer species of tree, and embellished by a unique rhododendron collection[5].

Historical relics in and near Balbirnie lend another flavour to the park. Reference has already been made to the Henge in adjacent Balfarg and to the Stone Circle near the North Lodge. Another marker of the past is the Stob Cross near the East Lodge, thought to have once stood at the entrance to St Drostan's Church, denoting sanctuary.

The first project in the new park development was the conversion in 1972 of the 18th century stable block into a Craft Centre. This created, round a cobbled courtyard, workshops and homes for craft workers, who at different times produced stained glass, jewellery and silverware, pottery and ceramics, knitwear, leatherwork, fashion and fabrics, models and furniture. Like many other Glenrothes ideas it became a model for others.

In 1980 a Caravan Site was completed in the south-east corner of the grounds by the Caravan Club of Great Britain, with the help of the Scottish Tourist Board. This provided spaces for 95 touring caravans. Some years later, Balbirnie Community Farm came into being, holding a variety of animal stock, demonstrating the virtues of organic gardening, and generally educating "townies" in the rural life.

Work started in 1979 on the conversion of the western half of the park into the town's second golf course, a challenging test, designed by a member of the British Association of Golf Architects. It was open for play in April 1983, but formally "hanselled" with a Show-Am tournament in 1984. (Some holes were later modified in deference to the less able/normal golfers!) For once the Corporation did not have to search for tenants; they arrived in the persons of the Markinch Golf Club who had lost their own course to wartime purposes. They became the Balbirnie Golf Club, and, trophies at the ready, moved into the new clubhouse which they had provided.

During the 1970s, however, the park seemed lifeless in that Balbirnie House

Participants in the 'Show-Am' tournament to mark the opening of Balbirnie Golf Course

lay forlornly empty and deteriorating, despite all efforts to interest potential users while maintaining the building in good order. Circumstances conspired to bring about a rescue. The Corporation persuaded Fife Health Board to take over New Glenrothes House, and itself moved into Balbirnie House in 1981. The necessary repairs and renovations, followed by its again being lived in, undoubtedly saved the House from sinking beyond recall.

In the years that followed, there were many expressions of interest in the building and eventually it was sold in 1988 for conversion to a hotel. Planning permission was soon obtained and the building re-opened as a 4-star hotel at the end of 1989, later opened officially by Mr Malcolm Rifkind.

Other Public Parks and Playingfields

From the 1950s Carleton, the town's first park, catered for a young population and for a variety of sports and public events, ranging from Highland Games to children's galas. It was the first home of the Glenrothes Cricket Club and later of the Rugby Club.

The 1950s also saw the development of playing pitches, bowling green and tennis courts at Dovecot Park, first under (the old) Kirkcaldy DC, and from

1961 under Glenrothes DC. In 1964 a pavilion was built and the newlyformed Glenrothes Junior FC moved into Dovecot.

The town was fortunate in having an area of great natural beauty in the valley of the River Leven. Glenrothes DC quickly decided to develop it into the main town park - Riverside Park. After a system of footpaths had opened up the area, it was largely left in its natural state, its attractiveness greatly enhanced over the years, mostly under the direction of Andrew Murray, by successive Councils. The Cricket Club moved in from Carleton.

The new Council also knew that every Scottish town worthy of the name must have its own golf course, and leased the Goatmilk area for the purpose. The course opened for full play in 1967 and the clubhouse followed shortly after.

Another landmark for the District Council was the completion in 1972 of Warout Sports Stadium. The Junior FC "flitted" from Dovecot to the main pitch. Several practice pitches, one all-weather, were provided next to the stadium. Warout was used for many purposes other than football. One particular event took place in 1982 - the World Pipe Band Championships, at which the massed pipes and drums played a specially composed lament for Alan McLure.

In the late 1970s, efforts were made to meet the needs of the western neighbourhood. A "community wing" was added to Newcastle Primary School in 1978, and in 1980 extensive facilities were provided at Glenwood School for shared use by the public. Kirkcaldy DC laid plans for Tanshall Park to have playingfields and a new bowling green. Though contributions towards the cost of a Sports Pavilion and all-weather tennis court were offered in the 1990s, the District Council was unable to go ahead before its demise.

Work started in 1992 on a 50 acre site at Gilvenbank[6], to give sporting and leisure facilities in the north. Space was allowed for shows or horse trials, tennis, bowls and two pavilions etc, plus the usual soccer pitches. Help was given in 1995 towards the cost of a top-class cricket square, and a joint pavilion for the Cricket and Rugby Clubs.

The Corporation's last major provision of this kind came in 1995, with the layout of playingfields at Lochty Park, and Atwal Enterprises sought permission for eight sports pitches with floodlights at Over Stenton.

Böblingen Way

From the 1960s, as the town expanded, there was gradually provided a system of walkways covering most of the area, and using where possible the line of the former mineral railway. In 1992, Böblingen Way was extended from South Parks Road to the Lomond Centre to cater also for bicycles. In 1995, the last two miles of paths were provided to complete the network for the town.

Social, Recreational and Cultural Facilities

From the start, the Corporation realised the need to provide premises for clubs and organisations. Tenants' meeting rooms were built for each precinct up to Caskieberran. The largest was at Woodside, formally opened on 14 January 1954, and still in regular use for many types of occasion. All were handed over in 1967 to the District Council, who also converted Balbirnie Woolmill for club use around the same time. In the later precincts, with money short, other devices had to be used, such as the conversion in 1980 of old farm buildings for Stenton Jubilee Centre, and a temporary building for Cadham.

Much of the early social and recreational life of the town revolved round the CISWO Recreational Centre. When the town was still to be mainly devoted to the housing of miners the Coal Industrial Social Welfare Organisation paid for the building of the Centre, officially opened on 28 February 1959. For many years, "CISWO" acted as town hall, housing such events as Art Exhibitions and Flower Shows. When the main hall was incorporated in the private Club in 1968, it was no longer open to the public for legal reasons.

In the late 1960s, the authorities together planned and financed the Fife Institute of Physical and Recreational Education, with a large multi-use sports hall, swimming pool, sports library, and other facilities, a major project of benefit to the whole region as well as the new town. The swimming pool was opened on 3 July 1970 by Emmanuel, later Lord, Shinwell. The Institute itself was formally opened by HRH The Princess Anne on 1 July 1971[7].

1979 saw the completion of the Lomond Centre in Woodside. This provided disco facilities and catered for a wide range of sports, hobbies and interests, including a recording studio available for hire, and a restaurant.

Rothes Halls

There was still a gap. From the earliest days there had been calls for a town hall, a theatre, some central facility. CISWO, the Woodside Hall, school assembly rooms, tenants' meeting rooms - all helped, but none gave a heart to the community.

Stenton Jubilee Centre

There was no shortage of plans. In 1965 the plan favoured was for a "Little Theatre". There was talk that, with similar backstage facilities, theatres in all the Scottish new towns could support a circulating repertory company. The "Little Theatre" was promised a grant of £10,000 by the Arts Council in 1966, out of a total cost of £40,000. Then it was felt that the building should be able to house musicals; the plan was revised; the cost was now £85,000.

In 1970 the District Council plaintively asked for something like the Byre Theatre, but by then several plans were in the air. In 1972 a working party was formed. There was an imaginative design for a theatre near the bandstand, overlooking Riverside Park. There was talk of the Technical College site. Agreement was finally reached on a plan for a complex in the town centre costing £400,000. Alas, Glenrothes DC vanished and then there was no money.

Perhaps all the angst was worthwhile. If any of these plans had come to fruition Rothes Halls would never have been approved.

In 1983 Loughborough Recreational Planning Consultants, an offshoot of the University of Technology, presented proposals for what was to become the

30 November 1993: Richard Wilson opens the Rothes Halls

The Rothes Halls

Rothes Halls. These were generally approved and the consultants were asked to prepare a design and model. Consultation and planning continued over the next few years, though it was clear that for technical and financial reasons the complex would have to await the start of the fourth phase of the town centre.

When the building finally appeared in 1993, it contained a large hall with retractable raked seating in moveable sections and portable staging; this could accommodate up to 1,000 for a standing performance, 950 for a formal conference setting, and 750 for a theatre setting. It contained also a smaller hall with theatre seating for 200, seven general purpose rooms, a library, ancillary accommodation, and the most high-tech facilities. The town at last had a heart, almost at the eleventh hour, and pioneers could hardly believe it.

First night was on 30 November 1993, start of the first St Andrew's Day Festival. After a "People's Pageant", the formal opening was carried out by Richard Wilson, the Scots actor/director. The first night performance included the Fife Fiddlers and the Tullis Russell Mills Band, with whom John Wallace, the trumpeter of international fame, who had started with them, played for the occasion. Hallelujah!

Citizen Glenrothes

A town does not automatically come to life through the provision of homes, and industry, and recreational and other supporting facilities. Still less can the public authorities breathe life into it. Only the residents themselves could give Glenrothes character. People came to the new town from a' the airts with their own customs and beliefs, hobbies and interests, hopes and ambitions. Often they came prepared to try new things; as often they brought social skills and experience from elsewhere.

In the 1950s and 60s there was much talk about "new town blues" throughout the UK. Luckily, Glenrothes escaped. This was due, partly to the way in which Glenrothes grew more slowly than other towns, and partly to the fact that so many residents came from the rest of Fife. That is not to say that the town escaped the ills which in later years beset British society. In 1980 the Glamis Centre was nicknamed "Little Chicago" because of the vandalism and gang warfare there. In the 1980s there were anxious meetings about the effects of drugs etc amongst young people.

Clubs and Societies

From the start Glenrothes had to build its own social life, and the new residents showed tremendous energy in setting up new clubs and societies,

and thereby fostering community spirit. Corporation employees were very active; for them it was almost an unwritten condition of employment.

One of the earliest bodies was the Community Association which from 1951 campaigned on all manner of topics, with bus shelters a specialty. W Stabler, Chairman, Jim Roger, Secretary, and his successor Ron Hutchison, took much credit for their efforts[1]. Other bodies early on the scene were the Horticultural Society (first show 1952), the Townswomen's Guild, the Children's Gala Committee, the Art Club, Badminton Club, British Legion, and a Juvenile FC.

Many other bodies followed over the years. Some gave particular service to the community, such as the Red Cross, Citizens' Advice Bureau, Rothes Rotary and Inner Wheel Clubs, the Round Table, Old People's Welfare Committee, YMCA/YWCA, and the various Residents' Associations. Others catered for special interests, such as the Cage Bird Society, the Camera Club, Floral Art, Slimline Club, Speakers' Club, and so on. There arose organisations for youth, for women, for a myriad sports.

Despite lack of facilities, drama prospered. In 1954 the Glenrothes Players put

Chapter

The Art Club and Floral Art Club exhibit in the Town Centre

on their first production "Castles in the Air" in the Woodside Hall. The Little Theatre Group won the Hunter Trophy in 1966 in the Annual competition of the Scottish Community Drama Association, with "The End of the Beginning". Two years later they narrowly failed to win the National Trophy[2].

In 1967, in its first venture, Glenrothes Musical & Operatic Society scored the first of many successes with "The Merry Widow" in Auchmuty school hall.

Churches

Many church organisations flourished strongly from the earliest years. It seemed that people coming from all over, making a fresh start in a new town, were ready to make a fresh start in the life of the Church.

"Operation Friendship" grew from an idea in the Youth Fellowship of the Rev Wallace Shaw in 1964, into international friendship exchanges of young people from the USA, Germany, Holland, Sweden, Ireland, England and Wales, with families in the host countries providing accommodation[3].

Other ministers and pastors became very much part of community life, among them Father McMeel who celebrated 25 years in Glenrothes in 1994. In 1995,

Operation Friendship delegates 1970 with Mr R S Watt, Deputy Chairman of the Corporation

73

Glenrothes is awarded the Council of Europe's Plaque of Honour September 1995

he became "Monsignor", an honour marked by his giving a celebratory Mass before Cardinal Winning, and a party in Rothes Halls attended by 450 people and addressed by the Cardinal. Much earlier, Glenrothes was the first new town to have a home missionary in the person of Ben Mills, a valuable asset from 1968 on.

Böblingen

The link between Glenrothes and Böblingen grew from a friendship between Fritz Metzger, rector of the Gymnasium there and Charles Anderson, a teacher at Glenrothes High. Böblingen is itself virtually a new town, rebuilt after almost complete destruction by wartime bombing. It lies in one of the most prosperous areas of Germany[4].

In 1970 Oberbürgermeister Wolfgang Brumme suggested a partnership between the towns. This was taken up in 1971 by the Corporation who decided on a formal twin link. "Show us your life, your thinking, and tell us your history and we will show you ours". Over the years that followed, there were contacts between the two towns at all levels - official, business, school, club and individual.

Young people from Glenrothes took part in a European Youth Festival at Böblingen Civic Centre in 1984. In the same year there was an exchange between the Böblingen Youth Symphony Orchestra and Tullis Russell Mills Band. The Choral Society and Fife Youth Orchestra went to Germany in 1985, the Fife Reel & Strathspey Society and YMCA in 1989. There was the exchange of sculptures already referred to. In 1995, gardeners from Kirkcaldy DC planted a rose garden in Böblingen for its garden festival the following year.

At a meeting in Böblingen in 1976 it was decided to set up the "Olympiad" movement, whereby the youth of the twin towns would gather every third year or so to compete in all recognised Olympic sports. This involved various other towns in Europe with which Böblingen was twinned, and the first Olympiad was held in Böblingen in 1978. The third, in 1984, was the turn of Glenrothes, opened by Princess Anne, and attended by 1,300 competitors and 150 leaders from towns in Germany, France, Holland, Italy, Norway and Wales. A large mural at Fife Institute commemorates the event, plus play features in the housing areas. 1995 saw the return of the event to Böblingen[5].

There was a special week of celebrations in September 1991 for the 20th

Princess Anne at Fife Institute with Adam Morley and Eileen Penny September 1995 –
25 years after she opened the Institute (photograph by courtesy of the Glenrothes Gazette)

Anniversary of the twinning. Glenrothes received a flag of honour from the Council of Europe[6] and there was a visit from the Musikkappele Dagersheim. In 1993 John MacDonald was awarded the Gold Medal of Honour in Böblingen for the personal energy and commitment he had brought to the town twinning. Martin Cracknell received the Cavalier's Cross of the Order of Merit for his services in strengthening business, cultural and social links between Scotland and Germany.

In October 1994 the Glenrothes Town Twinning Association was launched to co-ordinate the efforts of the various committees and groups involved in the Böblingen connection, taking over that function from the Corporation.

Sports

Participation in all manner of sports grew with the town. Cricket was early on the scene, driven by enthusiasts such as Louis Gordon. Rugby, like cricket, started in Carleton; it was with the Glenrothes club that Iain Paxton first came to prominence, through he had to move to Selkirk to be recognised internationally; Dave McIvor also started here before moving on to higher things; in the 1990's Paxton came back to coach the club and "higher things" began to move to Glenrothes. In 1969, Cy Harrison, boxing out of Balbirnie

Woolmill, became a champion and internationalist.

Football really "arrived" in 1964 with the formation of Glenrothes Junior FC. Under the able management of Andy Jack success was immediate - the Fife League Cup in their first season, the League championship the following year. They were narrowly beaten in 1968 by Johnstone Burgh after a replay in the Scottish Junior Cup Final. In 1975, now managed by John Forsyth, they made no mistake, winning 1-0 at Hampden against Rutherglen Glencairn. Unhappily, there was a dip in fortunes in later years, to the extent that a win in a minor competition in 1995 could be greeted by the headline "Shock Win for Glens" in the Glenrothes Gazette!

In October 1983, the first Glenrothes "Half Marathon" was run, won by Michael McCulloch of Grantown-on-Spey. This became a popular annual event. In 1988 the Corporation decided to sponsor Euan Henderson, the promising young snooker player.

Many individual and team successes flowed from the completion in 1970-71 of the swimming pool and Fife Institute. For example, Susan Martin became Scottish Junior Champion gymnast in 1985; Gary Watson was the first Scot ever to win a Gold Medal at the European Junior Swimming Championships. Minority sports also flourished, such as fencing, in which Valerie Cramb and Susan Paterson reached international status.

Local people with disabilities excelled in many sports at home and abroad, some taking part in international and Paralympic events. Iain Matthew won a swimming gold at the Barcelona Paralympics in 1992. He, along with Adam Morley, Paul Johnston, Anna Tizzard and Helen Lewis, to name only those from the Glenrothes Club, won medals at the European Championships in Perpignon in 1995. Most importantly, Fife Institute played a major role throughout the region in ensuring that sport is for all and not a lucky few.

Festivals, Games etc

Many clubs took part in the first Glenrothes Festival which was held 10th to 15th June 1963, a memorable occasion, ending in a Grand Parade through the town and a Ceilidh in CISWO. Unfortunately, the Festival dwindled and was abandoned in 1969. Highland Games were started in 1967 but also fell away. Sheepdog trials were more successful, and from the late 1960s onwards entertained large crowds for many years. However, a new series of Festivals of the Arts started in 1984, and of Highland Games in 1985.

Sir John Gilmour takes the salute at the World Pipe Band Championships 1982

Scott Meek, the first Glenrothes baby born in 1988, the town's 40th anniversary, is presented with his silver spoon

In later years, especially, there were all sorts of efforts to bring Glenrothes into the limelight. In August 1982, the World Pipe Band Championships were held at Warout Stadium, the scene also of the European Championships in 1984. In 1985, to coincide with the centenary of the Burns Federation, the first schools' contest for Burns songs and poems was held in the town. The Scottish Tourist Association held a Spring Flower Festival in March 1986; around the same time a Scotland/England international took place at the Fraser Bowl. June 1986 saw the first Open Aerobatics Championship at the airfield. In 1988 a Clothes Fashion Show was sponsored by the Corporation in the ill-fated Crystals Arena. Hot air balloonists set a new world record in 1991 when 10 craft were involved in the biggest ever linked take-off in the town park. Chess tournaments were held in Fife Institute involving world famous names.

Anniversaries

The town's interest in celebrating anniversaries grew as time went on. The 10th anniversary, 30th June 1958, of the town's designation was marked by a visit by HM the Queen. Though not strictly part of the celebrations, a significant event was the demolition by the TA in December, at the third attempt, of the massive Auchmuty Farm Silo, a landmark of pre-designation days.

By the 25th anniversary Glenrothes had passed a critical point in its development, but it was mostly left to clubs and societies to organise their own events if they wished. The Corporation, with the District Council's agreement, organised three evening receptions in the Falkland Suite[7] for representatives of all those felt to have contributed towards the growth and life of the town.

By the 30th, in 1978, the town was beginning to get the hang of this anniversary business. A week-long celebration took place, in which most of the clubs and societies took part. A brass band from Dagersheim near Böblingen lent international flavour to several events and memorably played in Lyon Square. Perhaps the most spectacular event, however, was the Scottish International Air Rally at the airfield.

The 40th anniversary in 1988 was celebrated in great style. On 1st July Prince Charles had a busy day, landing by helicopter on the riding-club ground near Leslie roundabout, unveiling the Good Samaritan sculpture in the town park, presenting prizes at Eastfield to the "Enterprise 40" competition winners[8], and attending the Highland Games.

Amongst other "40th" events, the BBC recorded its 100th edition of the "Antiques Roadshow" in the Fife Institute. Primary schools produced an exhibition showing the town through children's eyes, and also a book showing the town's history in cartoon form. There were charity football matches, an international cricket match, rugby sevens, aerobatics and aeromodelling championships, an international chess tournament including Boris Spassky, a Forty, Fit and Fabulous Festival, and so on. All babies born to Glenrothes mothers during the year were presented with a silver spoon bearing the Corporation crest; there were building society gifts to two infants born on the actual anniversary day; special anniversary cakes were distributed to geriatric wards in the hospital and to sheltered housing and similar establishments. The Churches combined in a Festival of Praise to mark the start of the week, and a town birthday party was held as a gesture of thanks to long term residents and representatives of the caring organisations.

It is to be hoped that, after wind-up in 1995, 30th June - the town's "Designation Day" - will continue to be celebrated in some way.

Glenrothes and Local Government

A question often asked about the new town was "When is it going to be a normal town?" - implying that it was in some way undemocratic. The answer was that in that sense it always was "normal". The normal local authorities operated within the designated area from Day 1; the Corporation was not a Town Council, and could not do what local authorities do. The Corporation was a development agency and depended on the elected authorities to provide the infrastructure and main and local services, just like anywhere else.

Reference is made in this book to various Councils and to those not versed in local government, the different types and their respective duties may be confusing.

The "old" authorities

The system in which the fledgling Glenrothes found itself was that set up under the Local Government (Scotland) Act 1929, largely consolidated in 1947. This gave a structure of county councils, counties of cities, large and small burghs and district councils.

The designated area came under the aegis of Fife County Council, which was an all purpose authority. In the early days the interests of the new town were looked after by George (later Sir George) Sharp, Councillor for Thornton, and William Cunningham, Councillor for Coaltown of Balgonie. Hard though they tried, they found it difficult at times to have the needs of Glenrothes recognised.

It was open to the county council at this time to create district councils within its area, composed of elected members for the relevant areas, and to delegate to them certain limited powers, mostly under the Physical Training & Recreation Acts. So it was that Glenrothes came within the ambit of (the first) Kirkcaldy District Council[1].

KDC Mark I

Initially, this "first" KDC was hardly enthusiastic about providing the new town with facilities. Though it laid out Bighty Park, it could not be persuaded in 1952 to provide a bowling green and tennis courts in Dovecot Park. In the following year there was created a "Glenrothes Recreational Facilities Advisory Committee", composed of representatives of the district council, the Community Association, the Coal Industry Social Welfare Organisation and the Corporation. The Committee did its work well, for in 1954 came an agreement whereby KDC undertook the Dovecot project, while CISWO - keen

Chapter **VIII**

to provide for incoming miners - undertook to finance similar facilities at the town centre. Beside these CISWO built its "Centre", officially opened in February 1959, and for many years virtually the "town hall".

The One-and-Only Glenrothes District Council

However, it became clear that the new "baby" was growing into too much of a handful for KDC, and in 1961 Glenrothes District Council was formed. This made sense, in that the new district council and the Corporation were concerned with the needs of the same area. Though they often disagreed, there followed more than a decade of productive co-operation between the two bodies.

Among those who came to prominence were Alan L McLure and Alex Devlin. The former was chairman of the district council for most of its life and also chairman of finance in the parent county council. The latter was chairman of Fife's education committee. When Alan McLure died tragically young, the Corporation chairman paid tribute to him as a formidable opponent but tremendous ally; his contribution to his adopted home town would never be surpassed; there were many monuments to his vision and dedication

Alan McLure

Other councillors whose names became associated with the town from this time included Bob King, who was to become the Chairman of (the new) Kirkcaldy District Council throughout its lifetime, as well as giving long service on the Health Board, Elizabeth Henderson, active in many spheres of the town's life; Jimmy Ferguson, long associated with the "Glens" football club; Pat Gemmell, one-man advice bureau to all in trouble. Messrs McLure, Devlin and King, and Mrs Henderson all served for periods on the Corporation also. So too did Mr Gemmell's widow, Vera.

Burgh Status

Perhaps it was because of the eminence of Messrs McLure and Devlin on the county council, and their ability to put the case for Glenrothes in that body, that the town never sought burgh status, but that is only speculation. There could well have been a town council at some point during the first 25 years under the legislation at that time[2].

At an early stage there existed a "Glenrothes Town Committee", bent on achieving burgh status. In 1957 they sought the Corporation's advice but were told that since the Sheriff would have to base his decision on an out-of-date census, it was very unlikely that he would grant a petition for burgh status.

Warout Stadium in 1972

The talk of burgh status revived from time to time and indeed was part of the platform on which the Scottish National Party fought the local elections in 1967.

Fife County Council

It followed that the Corporation had to depend on Fife County Council to provide most of the local authority services. Amongst these for the first 25 years was that of planning. In this respect Glenrothes was unique in that it was the only new town in the UK which did not have what was called a Special Development Order. This was an order passed by the Secretary of State conferring on a Corporation the status of planning authority for all the land which it owned or had previously owned. The Corporation complained regularly about the lack of an SDO but in fact had little to complain of at the hands of Fife County planners.

One thing is sure; the Corporation and District Council were not slow in making the town's needs known, even though they might sometimes be accused of looking rather far ahead; in 1952 the Corporation was trying to persuade the County Council that a crematorium was needed in the new town!

The main services provided by the County Council were education and social work, health and welfare (including cleansing), main roads and sewers. Fife showed itself far-sighted in the field of education. Schools were almost invariably provided in advance of demand so that new tenants moving into the town could find immediate places for their children in nearby schools. The only initial drawback was that senior pupils had to travel to Kirkcaldy, Buckhaven or Cupar for the later years of their education until the town justified a High School of its own. The opening of the first Glenrothes High School in 1966 was a landmark.

Another testimonial to the vision of the education authority and its Director of Education, Dr Douglas McIntosh, was the technical college. Dr McIntosh had travelled widely lecturing in the United States and was much impressed by the idea of a college laid out on the American campus principle. In the 1960s the County Council bought a large area of ground from the Corporation on which to build a series of colleges which would match the needs of the town and its industry as they developed.

The first Institute was polytechnic and the second was that of Physical Training and Recreation. Later, the college opened various other training centres in the town. In the 1990s the college reached the stage of providing Diploma courses which would count towards the first two years of degree courses at several Universities.

Before re-organisation, the County Council and large burghs of Kirkcaldy and Dunfermline together formed the Fife Fire Area Joint Committee and Fife Police Joint Committee. Until the early 1970s Glenrothes depended for fire cover on a part-time station in Markinch. Additional cover was then provided from converted buildings at the defunct Rothes Colliery, and a new fire station was built at Cadham. For a long time the police had to make do with a series of converted houses and shops, but in 1974 a new area police HQ opened in South Parks.

Re-organisation

In the 1960s the Government decided that local government in Scotland needed to be modernised. Following the report of the Wheatley Royal Commission, the Local Government (Scotland) Act 1973 was passed creating a new two-tier structure. Regional authorities were to provide those strategic services which needed to be co-ordinated over a wide area, along with major services requiring large resources. District Councils on the second tier would

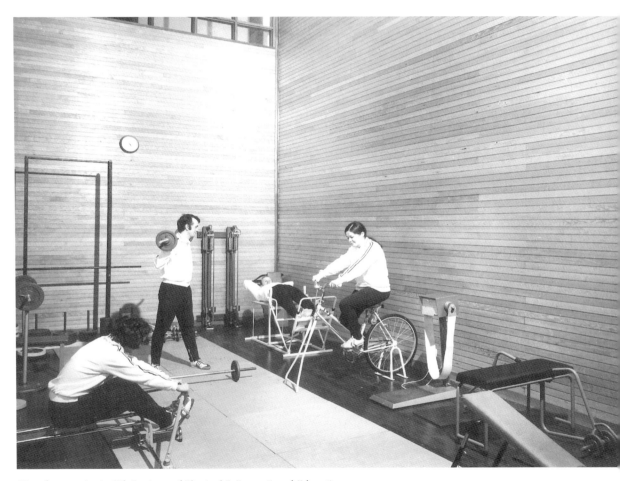

Time for exercise in Fife Institute of Physical & Recreational Education

have the task of caring for and improving the local environment.

A "Fight for Fife" campaign, championed by Sir George Sharp, had been successful. From 1975 Fife Regional Council was responsible for strategic planning, transportation and roads, police, fire, education and social work. A more muted fight for a Glenrothes District Council was not successful. (A new) Kirkcaldy District Council was responsible for local planning, local health and amenity, and housing.

Fife Regional Council

Fife - and Glenrothes - were fortunate, unlike most other areas of Scotland, that there was comparatively little upheaval as a result of re-organisation. The Region took the place in almost all respects of the County and the joint committees, and relations with the new Fife authority continued very much in the same good vein as before.

The most significant result of the re-organisation for Glenrothes was the decision by the new council on its headquarters. At a tense meeting in Kirkcaldy on 23 August 1974 the choice was between the historic county buildings in Cupar, various locations in Kirkcaldy, or Glenrothes. The

Corporation had offered to vacate Fife House[3] in favour of the Council, and that fact combined with the central geographical location of the town, swayed the decision in favour of Glenrothes. The cause of the new town was moved by Alan McLure and seconded by Pat Gemmell. In 1975 the Regional Council was able to move into Glenrothes. From then on, the new town was able to call itself "the capital of Fife"; this brought some wry comments from the more traditional minded.

Over succeeding years, further office blocks in the town centre were occupied by the Regional Council. In March 1988 they took over the former Burroughs site at Viewfield for the purpose of a new Police HQ for the Region. In the year of dissolution, after many deferments for financial approval, the new HQ was completed and occupied.

Along with re-organisation, the Secretary of State was persuaded that it was the right time to pass an SDO. In May 1975 came "The Town and Country Planning (Scotland) (New Town of Glenrothes) (Special Development) Order". This raised such a hullabaloo that, before it even took effect, Mr Bruce Millan had to present an Address to the Queen praying that the Order be annulled - a seal on the town's uniqueness!

One of the duties imposed on Regional Councils by the 1973 Act was to produce "Structure Plans" for their areas. Glenrothes came into the Plan for Kirkcaldy and Dunfermline. This was approved in 1983 and was favourably disposed towards the role which the new town had to play in the regional strategy. It did not, however, provide Glenrothes with a direct link to the national road network, but the Corporation's objections were not sustained. Nor was the Council willing to give priority to a Kinglassie bypass.

Kirkcaldy District Council (Mark 2)

From 1975, Glenrothes looked to the new KDC for local services, including planning. From the start, relations between the new Council and the Corporation were uneasy. That is not to say that local services such as parks and cleansing were not well administered in the new town. The Council took great credit for the gradually improving layout of Riverside Park, under the guidance of Andrew Murray. Planning control was put in place with great speed and efficiency under the chairmanship of Henry McLeish, before he was called to higher things.

Over the years there were in fact few major planning differences between the two bodies apart from the town centre expansion already mentioned. There

Residents enjoy Riverside Park

87

were problems from time to time over undeveloped sites within developed areas; though these had been reserved for later purposes, they were perceived by local residents as open or recreational areas.

The District Council was now responsible for producing "Local Plans". The Plan for the Glenrothes area, setting out a framework for the continuing development of the town and neighbouring communities, was adopted in 1990 and included the main components of the Corporation's own plan. A 1993 revision caused an objection about land use in the town centre, but this was resolved.

Officials of the two bodies kept up a close liaison. In 1991, with dissolution looming, this was formalised into regular meetings involving also members.

A Glenrothes District Council?

The main problem for Glenrothes from 1975 was the difficulty the District Council had in providing new social and recreational facilities for the town as it grew. This moved the Corporation Chairman to complain in 1989 that the residents were not being well served by KDC which saw its priorities as lying in the older parts of the district; by failing to provide new facilities the Council

had forced the Corporation to redirect government funding intended for economic development towards ends which the District Council was meant to serve. From two ends of the political spectrum Councillors Alan McLure and Douglas Mason accused KDC of neglecting the new town. In defence of the Council it was argued that the amount they were allowed to spend on capital projects was always severely restricted by the Government.

It is not surprising therefore that the Corporation looked to the Local Government Boundary Commission for salvation. Its interest in a forthcoming review of boundaries was registered with that body in 1985. The Corporation had no doubt that the establishment of a new authority to cater for Glenrothes and the neighbouring communities of Markinch, Leslie, Coaltown of Balgonie and Star of Markinch, would benefit not only the residents within the Greater Glenrothes area, but also the remainder of Kirkcaldy district. Consultants were appointed and their report was put to the Commission in 1986. Mr A H Martin, an Assistant Commissioner, met the Corporation in September 1988.

In May 1989 it was reported that the Commission had decided not to propose the formation of a new Glenrothes District Council. The view was forcefully put to them that local opinion should be sought through a public inquiry. In

September the Commission held a local meeting, at which the Corporation Chairman asked the Commission to reconsider. Though he was supported by Glenrothes Residents' Association and Glenrothes Residents' Council, the meeting was marred by in-fighting between the various residential groups.

In April 1990 the Boundary Commission, in response to the objections to its interim findings, acknowledged that no serious doubts had been expressed from any quarter and that Glenrothes was of a size and nature capable of sustaining a district authority. However, it was not their role to recommend change whenever it could be shown that a district council structure would be viable. Its proposals had to be made in terms which appeared to be desirable in the interests of effective and convenient local government. In response to calls for the setting up of a Glenrothes Council and suggestions that KDC claimed an inordinate share of resources, none of these sentiments seemed to the Commission to provide an adequate basis on which to sub-divide the relatively compact and convenient unit of administration that existed at present. For the Corporation it was a matter of regret that "party political advantage has taken precedence over the real issues about potential benefits of the people of Glenrothes". In November 1990 it was reported, to the surprise of no-one, that the Secretary of State had agreed to accept the recommendation that a separate Glenrothes District Council should not be formed.

Yet More Re-organisation

As things turned out, if a Glenrothes District Council had been created it would have been swept away only a few years later. People, even Corporations and Commissions, have great difficulty in knowing what is going on behind the face of government. With hindsight it seems reasonable to suppose that while Glenrothes was earnestly making its case to the Boundary Commission, it was well known in the recesses of St Andrew's House that change was on the way. In June 1991 a Scottish Office Consultative Paper appeared on "The Structure of Local Government in Scotland". This sort of thing does not appear overnight.

The Government's proposals were taking shape in 1992. While District Councils did not view their demise with equanimity, there was a great deal of support for the idea of a single tier authority for Fife, based in Glenrothes. From the viewpoint of the future wellbeing of the new town and the effects of wind-up, this seemed a good solution.

Aerial photograph of town looking westwards 1989

April 1995 saw the election of the shadow authority for Fife which would take over from Fife Regional Council in April 1996 under the new arrangements. Again Fife was fortunate compared with elsewhere in having so little disruption. District Councils would disappear, but the indication was that local services would continue to be administered locally. In light of the generally harmonious and helpful relationship with the new Fife Council's predecessors, it seemed that the new town could look forward to supportive local government after wind-up[4].

The Grim Reaper

On 28th October 1988 the Secretary of State issued his long-awaited consultation paper on the future of the new towns in Scotland, "Maintaining the Momentum".

General reaction in Glenrothes was that there should be some kind of body to continue the Corporation's work after wind-up. For example, industrial, commercial and housing assets might all be disposed of to a private company[1] (which might possibly be led by a nucleus of Corporation staff). Partial disposal to Glenrothes Enterprise Trust would make such a solution difficult. It was also felt desirable that a Glenrothes District Council be created, to which such things as landscaping might be handed over.

A Government White Paper "The Way Ahead"[2], issued in July 1989, promised a Wind-up Order in 1991, which would lead to the Corporation's being dissolved at the end of 1994. The Corporation saw that it had now two major tasks; first to complete the development programme already approved; second, to arrange for handover of its many assets and for the establishment of organisations to take over. Consultants were appointed and many options examined. There had to be arrangements for future development; for landscape, road and footpath maintenance; acceptable treatment of present tenants; and finance for infrastructure still needed.

The Scottish New Towns had to face a tougher challenge than their English counterparts, namely dissolution without a residuary agency[3]. There were inherent conflicts between development and asset disposal, and between pressure to sell and the need to keep a saleable portfolio. New forms of housing tenure had proved unacceptable to tenants. The capital programme, though adopted in principle by the Scottish Office, had run into funding difficulties.

The Order[4] when finally published in March 1992 gave 31st December 1995 as the date for wind-up; actual dissolution of the Corporation was to follow three months later. Detailed guidelines were slow to appear[5]. There was no truth in the suggestion by an anonymous wag in the office magazine that these said:

> *A great muckle roup ye maun haud,*
> *Your goods, graith and gear are to gae*
> *Wi a' your lasses and lads*
> *In December- oot in the snae.*

Fife Enterprise, Cadham, pledged to secure the town's future industrial growth after 1995

In June 1991 the final development programme had been confirmed. Talks were put in train with Fife Regional Council on such matters as the regional park, and with the district council on such matters as tourism. With the region there was set up a "Strategic Study of Greater Glenrothes" to examine long term land requirements and the prospects for future development as part of its Structure Plan Review[6].

Industry

There had to be a fundamental re-thinking of industrial strategy, taking account of the emergence of Fife Enterprise, to which responsibility for future economic development was to pass. By mid-1991 the idea of a local development company was receding, and the presumption against sale to sitting tenants was rescinded. The option of "management buyout" also came to nothing[7].

In 1992 the work of disposal started in earnest, and a plan of what was proposed was put to the Scottish Office[8]. It became necessary after all to refuse approaches by some tenants to buy their premises, so as not to fragment the available portfolio further[9]. In 1994, though the Corporation was still not selling units in Southfield, it was decided to include options to purchase in disposing of the estate.

One notable early success was the lease in February 1993 of various small workshop units to a newly formed Glenrothes Industrial Association[10]. The objective of this non-profit making body was to foster new and small businesses with a view to stimulating growth and employment in Glenrothes. This was seen as perhaps the best way of maintaining "life after death" of the Corporation.

Later in 1993, Whitehill and Viewfield industrial estates were sold as a single package to CTL Estates, Lancs[11]. In 1994 there was keen competition when Southfield was put on the market; it was sold to Allied London and Scottish Properties for £5.2M. Development land and some factory units at Bankhead and Southfield were bought by Fife Enterprise/ Scottish Enterprise. During the same year it was decided to transfer the Fife Food Centre to the Regional Council. With Scottish Office approval, this was done by way of a "balancing package", a method held up as an example for other new towns to follow.

At the end of 1994, after tenders had been invited, approval was given for the sale to Cinio Estates Ltd of the remaining Eastfield/Bankhead package. This was ironic in view of the town's early history, CINIO being a joint venture between British Coal Pension Funds and IO Group plc. Money from coal was at last helping Glenrothes!

Future Industry

In 1993, to help secure the future, the Corporation gave financial help to Fife Enterprise, and agreement was reached on a joint development programme for land at Bankhead and Southfield. Also in that year, with the encouragement of the Scottish Office, there was formed "Invest in Fife", a partnership composed of the Corporation, Fife Enterprise and the Regional Council, together marketing Fife. The idea was that this would provide a streamlined mechanism to attract inward investment, operating by pooling the resources and expertise of the three parties, and presenting a one-door customer-led approach to Locate in Scotland. It would have the potential to market Glenrothes beyond the life of the Corporation. Within the first two years of its establishment, the new organisation brought considerable investment into the area.

Also in 1993, the Government reviewed its policy on Assisted Areas. Glenrothes, as part of Kirkcaldy "Travel to Work Area", belatedly returned to

Saltire House is handed over, December 1990, to the Public Services Agency for the Inland Revenue

development area status.

Commercial

May 1994 brought the sale of Saltire Retail Park to New Land Assets, later passing to Prudential Nominees Ltd. In the same year, the "package" of neighbourhood shopping centres was sold to Allied London & Scottish Properties. The development site at Peploe Drive, Pitcairn was sold to Neighbourhood Centres (UK) Ltd.

Around the same time J Barr & Son were instructed to set a date for sale of the Corporation's equity stake in the town centre to CIS Ltd; the car parks would be included with a condition as to future public usage. The Bowling Alley, Forum, BP and Barnett's sites, and the Gala Leisure Centre were disposed of separately.

Public Housing

In the late 1980s, quite apart from wind-up of new towns, changes were brewing in the context of public housing tenure. At the end of 1987 a White Paper, "Future Housing Strategy", appeared and was widely publicised in the town[12]. New thinking was needed, new organisations created, home ownership pushed forward. The paper was discussed with Kirkcaldy District Council. The Corporation saw its first duty as being to its tenants, and as soon as all information was available, to have full consultations with the residents of the town.

The introduction of the Housing (Scotland) Act in 1988[13] led to the formation of Tenants' Associations in most precincts and a federal Residents' Council. A "Tenants' Participation Advisory Service" acted as independent advisers to the residents. Again there was as much publicity as possible throughout the town, the main object being to inform tenants about the alternative forms of tenancy which were to be available to them, and the legal implications. Few tenants were impressed. Consultants were appointed in December 1989 to advise the Corporation on the management and future ownership of its housing stock.

Discussions continued throughout 1990. The Secretary of State advised wide consultation; the possibility of transfer to some district council was not ruled out. The Scottish Office wrote to all Corporation tenants about their right of choice; judging by the findings of a survey throughout the Scottish new towns, they were still not impressed.

An early scene at the Fraser Bowl, latterly sold to the tenants

The formal handover of housing to the District Council

There was a second round of meetings with tenants' associations; the possibility of a Community Housing Association was mooted. Formal talks were started with Scottish Homes and various Housing Associations with a view to transferring vacant new houses to them. In October other options for house management were studied, such as the feasibility of Scottish Homes registering a non-property owning Community Housing Association, and "trickle transfer" of housing stock to another body.

In February 1991, the Scottish Office said that a) the role of local authorities would be decided once wind-up was in progress; b) the distinct issue of the authorities being managing agents was being considered. The Corporation could submit proposals on appointment of a Community Housing Association as a sole option. It was agreed however to encourage and respond to any initiatives put forward by Residents' Associations or their Federation, so that if possible tenants might later have a choice of landlord[14].

Guidelines for disposal of the housing stock were finally issued at the end of 1992. There was to be a ballot of tenants. The first task was to divide the town into ballot areas; these consisted of the 14 precincts with sheltered housing a separate 'constituency'. The District Council and other potential landlords[15] were invited to register their interest in acquiring the housing stock in all or any of the areas.

1993 was a year of consultation with tenants, potential bidders, and Scottish Homes. In January 1994 notification was received that the Corporation's proposals for the ballot were approved. An independent adviser, nominated by the Federation of Tenants' Associations was appointed. Consultants were engaged to help in the evaluation of bids.

In April 1994 bids were received from the District Council and interested Housing Associations[16]. After talks, however, it had to be arranged that these be re-submitted in September. A difficult process of evaluation followed, but the Corporation reported to St Andrew's House in October.

In December the Secretary of State approved the proposals, but with some re-adjustment. There had been amendment of the application of the guidelines on which the Corporation had based its conditions and on which those interested had made their bids, with a shift from VFM criteria to other factors. The Corporation had "no locus to agree or disagree and would not demur", but unless there was immediate advice or instruction a March ballot was thought to be impossible.

In the event, in March 1995, after an intensive publicity campaign, a postal ballot of tenants was held in each area, with the Electoral Reform Society acting as independent tellers. There was an impressive 80% response, and the result was a massive victory for the district council whose majority varied from 97% in Woodside and Auchmuty to 63% in Collydean. Only 3 persons voted against the council in the sheltered housing "constituency".

The result was greeted with some triumph by the District Council, who questioned whether the exercise had been worth the expense. The Scottish Office reply was that democracy was above price, and the tenants were entitled to a choice. Formal transfer of the housing stock followed, though not without computer and staff transfer problems which dragged on for months.

Other Housing

While all this was going on in the public housing sector, a determined effort was made to achieve completion of all private housing sites under construction. Nearing wind-up the town attracted many developers- a contrast

Community woodland passes to the Woodland Trust

with the early days. Sites of various sizes were sold at Formonthills, Coul, Leslie Mains and Balbirnie Burns.

Other forms of tenure also figured in the last few years of the Corporation's life. In particular, Housing Associations bought over 600 houses in new developments[17].

Landscaping and Woodlands

One of the wind-up tasks which was perhaps more difficult than listing bricks and mortar was that of identifying and evaluating those features of visual amenity which had been created as part of the town's inheritance, so that they could be passed on to other bodies.

A major achievement in 1994 was the transfer under Deed of Trust of 253 hectares of community woodland to the Woodland Trust, a private charity, with an endowment to ensure its long-term survival. Another 86 hectares at Formonthills passed to the Trust so that they could create a new forest park there; the lower slopes of the East Lomond would be restored to greenery after centuries of desolation. 10 hectares were planted by members of the public and school children during National Tree Week. In 1995, the Trust teamed up with Golden Charter, a funeral planning network, the first tree being planted under the scheme in May 1995 by Mrs Thomasina Davidson of Kirkcaldy. Well, it was the Corporation's "funeral" year.

The remainder of the town's woodlands and landscaped areas were transferred to the District Council on 31st March 1995, to be maintained in perpetuity, transitional arrangements having been made the previous year. Landscaping staff followed.

Community Related Assets

In 1993 a final report was sent to the Scottish Office on how the Corporation proposed to deal with the disposal arrangements for environmental, civic and community assets. The following year brought agreement for transfer of assets and liabilities to Fife Regional Council on a "neutral balancing package" basis from 31st March 1995. This included the foodpark, sites for future economic development, and feudal superiorities in private housing areas.

After 31st March 1995, the Rothes Halls passed to Kirkcaldy District Council, arrangements being made for an acceptable level of future revenue funding. The Council also took over community-related assets such as the public

convenience at Cadham, libraries at Woodside Way and Cadham, Stenton Jubilee Centre, Balbirnie Wool Mill, public halls and playingfields at various locations, the golf course at Goatmilk, Riverside Park, and the amenity areas in Balbirnie Park along with its overall control.

Many aspects of the town's social life were secured when premises were offered on favourable terms to clubs and voluntary organisations such as the Camera Club, Scout Groups, Tennis Club, Art Club and so on.

Corporation

Throughout the wind-up period, special arrangements had to be made with staff. For core or key workers, there were special inducements to stay. There was a general rundown of staff, both office and outdoor, and many over 50 took early retirement linked with redundancy. Staff morale was not helped when previously agreed severance terms were reviewed, and there was a period of work-to-contract. Nor did the Works Department always take kindly to contracts being put out to tender in accordance with Government legislation.

The task facing the staff must at times have seemed demoralising. All that had been put together since 1948 had to be analysed and re-assembled into packages for disposal. There had to be a "legal audit" involving examination of Titles held and deeds granted, an audit of land use planning submissions, a compilation of land information records and an environment audit, and so on. Consultants could help, but the basic work was "in house". Disputes with the workforce and delays in approvals did not help. Then came the very complicated practical and legal arrangements for disposal. Yet the timetable for wind-up was adhered to, and many of the systems devised became a model for other new towns.

Conclusion

By the time of the 1995 Annual Report the Corporation could say with confidence that the greater part of the wind-up process had been achieved. Industrial and commercial assets had almost all been disposed of; the local authorities had assumed their burdens; clubs and voluntary organisations had been provided for; contracts had been let for the final tidying up process, such as the Macedonia face-lift and the upgrading and completion of unadopted roads and footpaths; future development had been secured as far as possible.

By the end of the year, the last big hurdle - housing - had been cleared, and the Corporation could safely claim that it had carried out what had been required of it by the Secretary of State.

The Closing Chapter

"The Corporation .... now enters the period which is the beginning of its end. That fate, however, does not await Glenrothes; its future, as part of Fife and Scotland, is assured. For the town and its citizens it is the end of the beginning". So wrote the Chairman in the last report by the Corporation for a full year, 1994-95.

Before long the reign of the Corporation will be a fading memory. It is important therefore that knowledge of the town's origins and early history should be safeguarded. A pledge was in fact given that historical records relating to Glenrothes would be saved for posterity. Patrick Cadell, Keeper of the Scottish Record Office, was reported as saying, "It is wrong to think that records are just for historians. They are the raw material of our democratic rights as individuals". Unfortunately the Scottish Office papers prior to designation in 1948 had long since been destroyed. Archivists feared also a repeat of the destruction which followed the last local government upheaval 20 years before.

Arrangements were therefore made for the Corporation's archive to be transferred to Fife Council as a "residuary matter" and to that end liaison was established with the local authorities during the wind-up period. Preparations were made to ensure that all relevant computer data could be assimilated into the archive transferred. A photographic record of the Corporation's memorabilia was also prepared.

The Rocky Path

It would be easy to adopt a stance that Glenrothes succeeded despite all the difficulties put in its way and what seemed at times to be a lack of official support. Perhaps this is being over-sensitive; Government has to cater for a myriad competing demands, while at all times walking a financial tightrope.

From the beginning, also, there were Doubting Thomases who did not believe that the new town would ever succeed. There were others who resented its existence, believing that it would "cream off" public resources which might otherwise have been given to the older communities.

There were lingering regrets that development had been comparatively slow; that many hard won new industries had since left; that there had been near misses like Hewlett-Packard and VISA; that the sobriquet "Silicon Glen" had been hi-jacked; that the skilled and enthusiastic development team had to break up.

Chapter **X**

Corporation members & officials 1995 (Mr John W. MacDougall absent)

Dorothy Sayer is presented with the Rotary Club's 1995 Citizen of the Year Award; others commended are Richard Brickley, Alex Duthie and Tom McIntosh

There is no point, however, in pursuing these antique debates now. The important thing is that the difficulties inspired in those concerned with the town's development both a dogged determination to overcome the obstacles and also the ingenuity to get round them by diverse initiatives.

The Pioneering Spirit

There was an excitement, even idealism, amongst the early Corporation staff at the thought of creating a new world, nor did these feelings ever entirely evaporate. Picking out a few names does not belittle the contributions of many others. John Coghill and Bill Bodie were at the heart of the town's architecture and planning; Jack Baird and George Leitch were responsible for most of the housing between them, Alex Watson and Iain McLachlan for much of the industrial and commercial work. For most of the Corporation's life Alex Youngson masterminded the quantity surveying, and through it the building contracts. Engineers from George Sutherland to Andy Wyles designed most of the basic infrastructure, often on an agency basis for the local authority. *Si monumentum requiris, circumspice.*

Many others contributed, often above and beyond the call of duty. One of the highlights of 1995 was the staff reunion in December at the Rothes Halls.

Former and existing staff were given the chance to meet again during the last month of the Corporation's reign. No doubt some tales were told.

The pioneering spirit which inspired the early staff was present also amongst the townsfolk in general. People tried out new things - the Church, clubs and societies, new sports and hobbies. There was no lack of community spirit. On the night that the "Glens" returned *unsuccessful* from their first cup-final, it seemed that half the town had turned out to greet them. A vast crowd arrived for the opening of the airfield. There was tremendous support for all the town anniversaries. It was the same spirit which caused Alex Duthie, 1995 winner of a Clydesdale Bank's "Time of Your Life" award, to ask that his prize of £1,500 go to the town's Age Concern.

Dulcius ex asperis

Necessity is the mother of invention. Innovation was a key word in the history of the town's growth. Glenrothes pioneered the creation of Scotland's "Silicon Glen", laid the first new town airfield, joined what was at the time a unique combination of three authorities to produce a Sports Institute, created the GUID Club, and so on. Even at the end, it was Glenrothes which led the way in devising procedures to solve the problems of wind-up.

The 'last piece of the jigsaw' – the Western Distributor Road is opened October 1995

103

Sir Hector McNeill
1948 - 52

Sir Garnet Wilson
1952 - 60

Lord Hughes
1960 - 64

A virtue was also made out of necessity as far as the Corporation offices were concerned. When it was known that the Electricity Board was looking for premises in the town, they were offered the "hutted encampment" at Woodside, and the Corporation was allowed to build and move into what became Fife House. When local government reorganisation loomed, Fife House was offered to the Regional Council, and the Corporation moved again, this time to Glenrothes House. When the Health Board was looking for a home and Balbirnie House desperately needed to be occupied, Corporation staff moved into the latter and various other locations. Finally, when the time was right to attract a top-class hotel into Balbirnie, the former Haig's offices were available for the last move. It was all in a good cause.

One of the criticisms levelled at "quangos" is their secretive nature, with meetings held behind closed doors. In 1986 the Corporation took the historic step of opening its meetings to press and public, in the same way as elected bodies. Even though commercially sensitive matters had to be discussed in private, it was a great advance. In recognition of this initiative, the Corporation was in 1988 given an award by the Campaign for Freedom of Information.

From 1985, the Corporation came under the eagle eye of the local government Ombudsman. Though several complaints were taken to him, he decided that none of them amounted to "maladministration"[1].

The Authorities

The growth of the town from 1948 to 1995 worked best when there was a smooth-working partnership between the County/Regional Council, the Corporation and the District Council of the time. The contributions of the latter were most obvious in the social and recreational facilities, when they were able to provide them. The contributions of Fife Council were inestimable. Apart from the continuing services such as education, fire, police and social work, they provided much of the basic infrastructure which is either unseen or taken for granted such as main roads, drainage and water, usually in pace with the town's development. The town had survived two local government upheavals with hardly any interruption.

The Corporation was not always the most popular of animals. In the early days there were public protests about such things as house rents, which were always higher than those for comparable local authority houses. As often as not the protests were led by Alan McLure who otherwise gave so much positive support to the town.

In the latter days there were the problems of wind-up, which was seen, in the words of the Chairman as "an objective worthy of our best endeavours". Even though it had always been known that the Corporation would sooner or later be wound up, some very fundamental thought had still to be put into the wind-up process, not only in order to smooth the transition, but also to provide as well as possible for the future within the inevitable restraints. In this the local authorities played a major part.

Personalities

The Corporation had a series of remarkable Chairmen. After the all too brief reign of Sir Hector McNeill, the Board was chaired by Sir Garnet Wilson who brought business experience and rich humour from Dundee; there followed another ex-Lord Provost of Dundee, Lord Hughes, whose business and political skills took him on to higher things; then came R R Taylor with his industrial and diplomatic expertise; he was succeeded by Sir George Sharp, "Mr Fife" himself, whose name is writ large over so many aspects of Scottish local government from the 1940s onwards; finally from 1987 to 1995, came Professor Kit Blake who brought high intellect and commonsense to what was

in many ways the most difficult phase of the town's growth.

Also on the Board[2] for periods were Conveners and other members of Fife County/Regional Council who gave weighty support and encouragement, such as John Sneddon, Sir John McWilliam, Robert Gough and John MacDougall. Mention has already been made of the contribution of members who came to the fore in successive District Councils. Of these none had a closer connection with Glenrothes than Bob King, who was one of the first building workers who came to work in Glenrothes in 1950 and moved into the town with his family in 1954, and who was the only Provost of Kirkcaldy District Council from inception in 1975 to dissolution in 1996. For most of the second and third phases of the town's development, the Corporation's efforts were led by Chief Executives "Paddy" Doyle and Martin Cracknell.

Glenrothes fell within the parliamentary constituency of Central & West Fife and boasted two prominent MPs. Willie Hamilton, much maligned for his anti-royalist views[3], and fearless in tackling the establishment generally, represented the area for many years. No doubt his outspoken-ness had something to do with the fact that he was never promoted. Henry McLeish played for the "Glens" and later East Fife FC, before going on to more serious

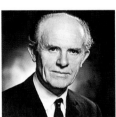

R R Taylor
1964 - 78

Sir George Sharp
1978 - 86

Prof. C Blake
1987 - 96

105

things, first with the local authorities and then in Parliament. At the end of the period, as a Shadow Minister and with Labour odds-on favourites to win the next General Election, he looked set for high advancement.

The Legacy

By the end of 1995, the Corporation's legacy was a town with a population of just over 40,000 (around 50,000 if one takes in the nearby villages), well provided with housing, industry, educational and commercial facilities, social and recreational outlets, roads and other infrastructure, woods and landscaping, all within comfortable distance both of the main cities of Scotland and the best of its countryside. Everything possible had been done to hand over this legacy in good shape to the authorities and other organisations who were honour bound to continue the good work.

Those responsible received an unsolicited testimonial in 1995 in the annual report of the Glenrothes Federation of Tenants' and Residents' Associations. A spokesman was reported as saying, "It has been with pride that we have escorted visiting delegations from other new towns around Glenrothes. We undoubtedly live in the most beautiful of the new towns in Scotland, if not Britain". Surely the town had achieved the status of "A Garden City of Tomorrow".

31 December 1995 was the end of the beginning. From 1 January 1996, the title "New Town" could no longer apply to Glenrothes. Few would deny that, with all its human, environmental and locational advantages, it was set to remain a major growth point in the Scottish economy, or that, with its strong community identity, it is now an integral and vibrant part of the ancient Kingdom of Fife.

NOTES

Chapter I

1. See "The Fife Coal Company: A Short History" by Augustus Muir.
2. In fact, ahead of Glenrothes, a new town near Lochgelly actually reached the stage of Cabinet approval.
3. Apart from Westwood and Glenrothes, others suggested included Auchmuty, Ballenbreich, Cadham, Dalginch, Glenore, St Drostan, and Sythrum. Even after the choice was made the name "Glenrothes" was not universally popular, and grumbles echoed on for some time. After registering the birth of their daughter, one of the Corporation drivers, Arthur Anderson, told his wife that the birth was the first registered under the new name Glenrothes. It was the same Mr Anderson who carved the Coat-of-Arms on the first piece of coal to be brought to the surface at Rothes Colliery, and also a wooden gavel for Corporation meetings.
4. In the 1990s a belated comfort to his shade was the naming of Westwood Park in Bankhead.
5. Draft New Town (Glenrothes) Designation Order 1948: Memorandum by the Secretary of State for Scotland: January 1948: Department of Health for Scotland: pub HMSO.
6. See Report of Proceedings at A Public Enquiry held within the County Offices, Wemyssfield, Kirkcaldy on Wednesday, 31March 1948 before Mr J R Philip OBE KC, Commissioner ref DE 1919/1.
7. See New Town at Glenrothes, Fife: Explanation of Proposal Review of Objections and Secretary of State's Decision: Department of Health for Scotland: 30th June 1948: pub HMSO.
8. New Town (Glenrothes) Designation Order 1948, made under New Towns Act 1946 Section 1.

Chapter II

1. See "Some Light on the Past Around Glenrothes" and "Glenrothes & Its Environs in Days Gone By" both by W G R Bodie. As well as being principal planner of the town's development for the first 20 years or so, Bill Bodie pioneered research into the area's history.
2. See "Scotland - Archaeology & Early History" by G & A Ritchie; "Balfarg: The Prehistoric Ceremonial Complex" by Gordon Barclay.
3. See "The Auld Toon o' Leslie" by Andrew Hunter.
4. While the Leslies of Rothes and Balfours were predominant part of the south-east of the designated area was owned by the Leslies of Balgonie, and of the south-west by the Aytoun family before it passed to the Balfours. See plan at Appendix I.
5. Old Statistical Account of Scotland 1791.
6. New Statistical Account of Scotland 1845.
7. See "Historical Records of the Family of Leslie" by Col C Leslie; "Grip Fast: the Leslies in History" by Alexander Leslie Klieforth.

8. The Rothes papers were handed over by the Corporation to Kirkcaldy Museum for safe-keeping, passing in course to Fife Council.
9. "History of Tullis Russell & Co" by C D M Ketelbey. See also Rothmill Quarterly Magazine, the works magazine of Tullis Russell & Co, 1933 onwards.
10. For an excellent account of industry in the area generally, see "The Past at Work around the Lomonds" and "Social Conditions around the Lomonds, 1775-1875" by G P Bennett, author also of "The Great Road between Forth and Tay".

Chapter III

1. At the height of the Cadco crisis the Secretary of State decided to strengthen the Board by appointing an extra member with industrial background - Mr J B Rae.
2. The Scottish new towns put forward the case more than once that they should be allowed to borrow temporarily on the "money market", to tide them over periods of high interest rates. With much expenditure in its earlier years at lower interest rates, East Kilbride was eventually to show a "profit" on current operations, but none of the other Scottish new towns, including Glenrothes, was able to reach that level of achievement.
3. "Official" history can be seen in the Annual Reports of the Scottish New Towns from 1948 onwards: HMSO. See also "A History of Glenrothes": Keith Ferguson (1982) and "40 Years New Glenrothes 1948-1988": Alistair J D Wood; "Glenrothes Bulletin" 1952-66; and the "Grapevine" 1972-95. The town was truly recognised as such with the creation of its own newspaper, and full chronicles are contained in the columns of the Glenrothes Gazette, Leslie & Markinch News from 21 November 1962 onwards.
4. At an early stage the Corporation guaranteed to meet any shortfall of rateable return in relation to local authority expenditure on the town. The guarantee was never taken up.
5. Ironically, the official who received him was George Young who went on to be a most successful Chief Executive of East Kilbride Development Corporation.
6. The closure roused great controversy, the public having become attached to the South Street shops. The latter were converted for some years to other useful purposes, such as another staging post of the Police HQ.
7. The novel design, much modified (against the wishes of the architects) to meet planning and building byelaw reservations, was unfortunately likened to a draughty railway station.
8. The Golden Acorn (now the Albany Hotel) became a great favourite with townspeople for many years, contrary to the prediction of many who christened it "Armstrong's Folly" after the Brewers' executive who masterminded it.

NOTES

Chapter IV

1. Central Scotland: A Programme for Development and Growth: 1963: HMSO Cmnd 2206.
2. Dr J Dickson Mabon was the Minister in charge at the Scottish Office of a policy to boost housing production by industrialised methods. He was also closely involved in the investigation of the Cadco affair (below).
3. These were to have been in small culs-de-sac next to the A92 in Pitteuchar.
4. The first meeting of the GUID Club was on 19 November 1968. The idea was first floated at a conference at Glenrothes held by the Edinburgh & Dist Branch of the BIM on "Mutual Support - University & Industry". Mr J Steven Watson, then Principal of St Andrews, proposed the setting up of a Dining Club at which academics and industrialists could exchange views. It would be the "Scottish 20th Century version of the 18th century Lunar Society". Many of the benefits were intangible; others which germinated in the Club included a special masters degree course, training attachments, liaison on recruitment, consultancies and co-operation on R & D.
5. Report by Board of Trade Inspectors on Cadco Developments Ltd etc: HMSO.
6. See "Blood on the Walls" by Willie Hamilton.
7. Report on a Public Inquiry: P Bonsell: 1979.

Chapter V

1. In fact the growth target identified in the "Profile" was not achieved, a shortfall of about 1000 houses equating roughly with the population shortfall. It is probable that the date rather than total population was uppermost in the Secretary of State's mind.
2. In October 1991 the Corporation Chairman wrote to St Andrews House supporting the Fife case for assistance, emphasising the loss of funds in the area through the Corporation's impending wind-up.
3. The premises were severely damaged by fire in 1985 and eventually became the site of the new Fife Police HQ.
4. In 1995, with Barr Thompson itself gone, outline planning permission was granted for redevelopment of the site as a bingo hall and fast food restaurant.
5. Glenrothes products went far and wide, as exemplified by Spandrel Orbits (alas no more). After building the home for the Tudor warship Mary Rose, they moved in 1982 to building lightweight frame hangars for the Falklands (four ready for shipment in 9 days); their products also went to Newport, Rhode Island, to the Offshore Exhibition in Aberdeen, to several ceremonies on the Papal visit to the UK.
6. In 1986 Thermaflex won the Queen's Award for Export Achievement, followed in 1992 by Coors Ceramics and Compugraphics International. In 1992 Liquid Lever Innovation Ltd won the John Logie Baird Award and their Managing Director Nigel Buchanan the Glengoyne Award both for innovation.
7. The Crystals Arena, built in the early 1980s, was for several years a popular venue for ice sports and indoor bowling, but then ran into severe financial difficulties, and all attempts to find someone to take over failed.
8. In 1995, Beckman's having moved to Eastfield, work started on a Safeway supermarket on their site, and so a symbol of the town's success which had stood since 1958 at the entrance to Queensway Industrial Estate and given its name to the roundabout, was lost.
9. The competition brought a massive world-wide response. A panel of judges picked by the Royal Aeronautical Society chose a Mr Stephen Cannon as the winner, with his project for equipping aircraft interiors. Four other awards were made. Over the next two years the airfield was improved, buildings were altered and occupied, an existing unit was adapted to form terminal and club facilities.
10. Even so, by 1995, there was still a large gap between the supply of (14%) and demand for (40%) single person accommodation, demand almost equalling that by family applicants. Changing times!
11. Thus groups of houses in Balfarg, Collydean and Finglassie, were sold 1990-93 to Kingdom Housing Association, another in Stenton 1995 to Hillcrest HA.
12. Against the tide of depression in the cinema industry, the Corporation had from the earliest years tried to attract a cinema, but the town had then to make do with a film club and the occasional showing in the Woodside Hall, with the option of going to Leslie and Kirkcaldy.
13 Apart from Fife House and its various extensions, and Glenrothes House, other developments included North House built by Fraser & Co, Hanover Court by Melville Investments and Heritage House by Messrs Joseph Smith.
14. In 1995 an English specialist in highway claims appeared on the scene, trying to interest those affected in pursuing the highway authority for depreciation in the value of their property.
15. For a statistical summary of the position reached by the end of 1995, see Appendix II.

Chapter VI

1. "Bodie's Boulders" were nicknamed after William J Rowntree Bodie, principal planner for the first half of the new town's life. With each development he insisted on the contractors depositing any large boulders unearthed so that they could be used as landscape features.
2. See Chapter IX. In their first year, with public involvement, the Trust planted 30,000 out of 80,000 trees at Formonthills, and the community woodland was already beginning to take shape.
3. Sponsored by the Arts Council, the sculpture was both unusual and

attractive, and might have succeeded in another time and place. The sculptors were Jenny and Stephen Scott.

4. See "Balbirnie Park, Glenrothes", and "Balbirnie Park, Visitors Guide", pub 1984 and 1991 respectively by GDC.

5. Many of the rhododendrons were introduced from about 1850 from the Himalayas by the noted plant collector Sir Joseph Hooker, through George Balfour who worked in India 1841-67, latterly as a judge, and whose wife was Hooker's niece. The credit for recognising the importance of the collection and ensuring its survival largely belongs to the late Andrew Cassells, advised by H H Davidian of Edinburgh Botanic Gardens. A painting "Rhododendron Arboreum" by Stella Turner was presented to Davidian as a tribute. A booklet by Cassells on the collection is unfortunately out of print.

6. Many of the social and recreational facilities described were financed either partly or wholly by the Corporation. For much of the Corporation's life grants were made under a "Major Amenity" allowance, often of one-quarter or one-third of cost, to enable local authorities or others to carry out projects. Often the basis of such aid was that it was used to finance the first phase of a project, leaving the authority to complete the project at some later unspecified date. This led the Chairman, on the occasion of the Gilvenbank project, to emphasise that the Corporation was not required to provide such facilities as this was a district council responsibility, and say in the "Grapevine", "Over the years we have gone well beyond our legal obligations. Throughout the town we have either created or assisted in the creation of a very wide range of such facilities, but the extent of our activities is not often appreciated by the citizens. At the northern area alone we have put a substantial amount of resources but we are still being asked to do more". After detailing the many types of social and other facilities provided, he went on, "Now at Gilvenbank we are creating, entirely without assistance, a very substantial community asset with, so far, rather less public recognition than we deserve".

7. In September 1995, now the Princess Royal, she visited the Institute to unveil a plaque celebrating the completion of a new artificial grass area, and to commemorate the Institute's first 25 years.

Chapter VII

1. In 1953-54 the Corporation published a series of Newsletters for tenants, full of friendly advice and practical information about house maintenance etc. This preceded the Glenrothes Bulletin (1955-66) produced by the Community Association, and gives a fascinating insight into the concerns and interests of residents in these early days.

2. In 1958 Forsyth Hardy of "Films of Scotland" suggested making "New Day", a film showing the prosperity of the area as a result of the Rothes Pit and new industries. Glenrothes Players supplied the cast; Jimmy McMillan played the miner in the story and Louie Walker, his wife. The film was used for years to promote the town until overtaken by events.

3. This was pioneered by YF members such as Ian Sloan, Douglas Brodie and Alex Pattison and sustained over the years by volunteer organisers such as Dorothy Sayer, Joy Allan, Lilian Sloan and Doris Murray. In 1995 Glenrothes entertained youngsters from the Netherlands and 10 local members visited Prague; Operation Friendship celebrated its 30th anniversary on 7 October with a mini Olympics for youngsters and a dinner/dance in the Lomond Centre.

4. Böblingen lies southwest of Stuttgart in the State of Baden Wurttenberg. After the Allied bombing almost the only building left standing was the parish church. In March 1986 Glenrothes representatives attended the retiral ceremonies for Oberbürgermeister Brumme. In 1995 Kirkcaldy District Council held a reception for representatives of all the twin towns within the District, which was destined to disappear in the 1996 re-organisation. Oberbürgermeister Alexander Vogelsgang attended from Böblingen.

5. Other Olympiads were held in Pontoise in 1981, Geleen in 1987, Alba in 1989 and Krems in 1992. While the objectives were the making of friendships with those from the other twin towns and the forging of team spirit, the Glenrothes representatives did not neglect competitive success. In 1995, 180 participants brought back 34 gold, 34 silver and 26 bronze medals, matching Germany. Much of the success of the Olympiad venture was due to Jim Penman of the Fife Institute and its team of coaches.

6. The "Plaque of Honour", the Council of Europe's second highest award, was given to the town in September 1995 in recognition of outstanding achievements in town twinning and related European affairs. This was presented in Rothes Halls and marked by a parade of uniformed organisations from St Columba's Church to the Halls.

7. The Falkland Suite was a suite of rooms above the Royal Bank of Scotland, which was sublet by the bank for some years and adapted for public exhibitions, functions and club activities etc. It proved very useful.

8. The "Enterprise 40" competition was designed to enable entrepreneurs aged 40+ to launch their own businesses in Glenrothes. The judging was chaired by James Gulliver.

Chapter VIII

1. By a quirk of boundaries part of the western area of the town came under Lochgelly District Council, but the effect of this was imperceptible.

2. The first Scottish new town, East Kilbride, had "small" burgh status for many years and then by special Parliamentary procedure became a "large" burgh. In the 1960s Cumbernauld also became a "small" burgh.

NOTES

3. Initially, when occupied by the Corporation, Fife House was known as "Glenrothes House". The Corporation's next home was called "New Glenrothes House", though "New" was later dropped from its name.

4. Fife Regional Council finalised its Structure Plan in October 1992. This replaced the previous Plans for N E Fife District and the combined Dunfermline/Kirkcaldy Districts. The functions of the new Plan, inter alia, were to set out strategic policies and major proposals for the development and use of land and to provide a framework for the production of local plans. Observations on Glenrothes included the following:-
"The strategy for Glenrothes is to continue its role of attracting industry and services, hence generating employment opportunities and meeting private housing demand...The strategy for economic development is to ensure that existing industrial sites are marketable. Particular importance is attached to...the Bankhead area...and aviation related businesses....Glenrothes is to continue to be a major focus for residential development. ...The town's role is seen as serving the shopping needs of the immediate hinterland. There is a need for further car parking...improvements to the A92 between Preston and Balfarg...are required".
Only the remark about serving the shopping needs of the immediate hinterland seemed to contain the seeds of future dispute, if ever further extension of the town centre were needed.

Chapter IX

1. A "Thamesmead" type of solution was considered. In Thamesmead, under a pioneering initiative, a Trust had taken over the commercial and industrial assets as well as the former GLC housing stock. Most members of the Trust were elected by residents and members of the public though they had no voting rights.

2. "The Scottish New Towns: The Way Ahead": IDS July 1989: HMSO Cm 711. This followed an independent survey of tenant opinion throughout the new towns. The Government's views conflicted with those of SLANT, the forum representing Scottish local authorities with new towns, which pressed for all services to be transferred to the relevant councils on wind-up, with extra funding from central government. The White Paper was said to reflect the Government's belief that the Scottish new towns were more important to the Scottish economy than their counterparts in England and Wales. One person in twenty in Scotland lived in a new town and they had succeeded in attracting over 30% of all jobs created by inward investment. The major emphasis in housing was to be on increasing choice in the rented sector. Industry should pass to a private sector based local development company and the Government would welcome "soundly based management buy-out proposals". Planning in the other

new towns would change to the Glenrothes pattern, in that Special Development Orders would be revoked at the time of dissolution. The skills of Corporation staff should be preserved by their being privatised wherever possible.

3. England and Wales had a New Towns Commission which took over residuary assets as each new town was wound up.

4. The New Towns (Glenrothes) Winding Up Order 1992 SI No 354 (S.28). Winding up was to begin on 1 March 1992 and reports on progress had to be made as at 31 March each year. The Corporation had to comply with any directions made by the Secretary of State.

5. When these finally appeared they dealt with the successor arrangements for economic development, disposal of industrial assets and housing transfer ballots and sale. The process would be strictly monitored and approval would be needed for any disposal of property valued at £250,000 or more. The Chief Executive was appointed as the Corporation's "accounting officer". This meant that he had to emphasise the financial criteria when advising the Board, rather than the best socio/economic solution.

6. See note 4 to Chapter VIII.

7. A Working Group was set up to assess any submission and guard against conflict of interest. At the end of the day the ground-rules laid down by the Scottish Office for contracting out functions to former staff members proved to be too rigorous for those interested.

8. In October 1991, a report on the expected Wind-up Order had highlighted the lack of guidance from St Andrew's House and the shortness of time to liquidate rights and responsibilities. By December there was still no date for the Order, but all had still to be achieved as laid down!

9. Consultants reported in March 1993 on sale of remunerative assets such as industrial estates and mortgages, share of town centre equity etc.

10. The Board of Management came from local industry, commerce and the public sector. In its first year it was on schedule to buy instead of leasing; it had dealt with 171 enquiries and created 30 new tenancies; in 1995 it did buy.

11. The last major tenant in Viewfield, BICC Brand-Rex bought their premises in 1994 and in 1995 bought the former Crystals Arena for expansion.

12. This contained the Government plans for the future framework of housing policy in Scotland. There were four main objectives:- a) to continue to spread home ownership as widely as possible; b) to revitalise the independent rented sector; c) to encourage public housing authorities to change and develop their role; d) to use money more effectively so that tenants were given a better deal and so that the role of the private sector was increased. New Town Corporations were to continue to promote home ownership, let houses to those who do not want to buy and provide

more housing for special needs. However, tenants were to be given the right to transfer to other landlords and Corporations encouraged to dispose of housing in advance of wind-up to a range of alternative landlords.

13. The 1988 Act also brought Scottish Homes into being, a body which in the event played little part in housing disposal, contrary to Government hopes.

14. Also in February 1991, there appeared a report of a Joint GDC staff and Tenants' Federation Working Group - "Our Homes: Our Vision - Vision II Reality". Given the current lack of information from the Government, it was strongly recommended that GDC make no decision on establishment of any town-wide management agency at this stage. They wanted to "develop a collective vision of where we want to be in 1994 rather than attempt to unravel the mysteries of the various organisational structures". In December 1992 the Federation produced a further paper "Joining Together: A Strategy for the Future", which was at odds with official views.

15. These had to meet certain standards and be registered with Scottish Homes.

16. The Corporation had reservations about the timetable which had been set by the Scottish Office, unless the latter responded within a specified period. The bodies which finally opposed Kirkcaldy District Council in the ballot were Collydean Community Housing Association for Collydean; Glenrothes Community Housing Association for Rimbleton, South Parks, Caskieberran, Macedonia, Tanshall and Newcastle; Hillcrest Housing Association for Woodside, Auchmuty, Pitteuchar and Stenton; and Kingdom Housing Association for Cadham, Pitcoudie and Balfarg.

17. Kingdom Housing Association bought 140 houses in Balfarg and 29 in Collydean; Link bought 30 in Finglassie; Hillcrest 216 in Stenton; and Collydean Community Housing Association, a total of 190.

Chapter X

1. In this connection it is perhaps worth noting a Customer Care Mission Statement by the Corporation in 1993, fathered by John Major's "Citizen's Charter". This ran - "The Corporation recognises the important contribution that customer relations make to the effective provision of a public service. It sets out to establish a commitment to achieving, within its financial constraints, the highest possible standard of customer care provision to all those to whom it provides a service both outside and within the Corporation. To this end it will endeavour to provide the leadership, training and working environment which will enable all its employees to assist the Corporation in achieving that commitment".

2. Complete lists of Corporation members and of Chief Officers and Heads of Department are annexed at Appendix III.

3. The press, however, had great fun when Mr Hamilton was introduced to the Queen in Fife House in July 1982. Both survived.

LIST OF ILLUSTRATIONS

Front & back Endpapers: Part of "Doing Things", the record-size mural painted by Glenrothes school children on the hoardings around the Phase IV extension to the Town Centre

LIST OF ILLUSTRATIONS

(Where not otherwise stated most of the photographs shown were commissioned over the years from Mr A L Gordon and Harvey Photography Ltd, whose work is gratefully acknowledged by the Corporation).

APPENDIX I

"Land Ancestry in Glenrothes"

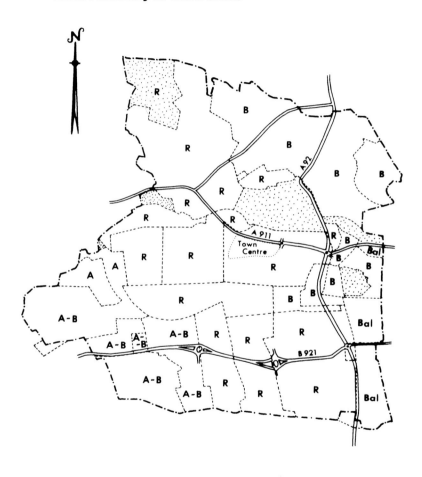

R	= Rothes	Bal	= Balgonie
B	= Balfour	A	= Aytoun

Map of major land acquisitions

APPENDIX II

STATISTICAL SUMMARY AT 31 DECEMBER 1995

Population and Housing	Estimated population		40,250
	Corporation built dwellings		12,806
	Housing Associations		109
	Privately built		2,463
	Total		15,378
	Owner Occupancy Rate		64.3%
New Industry	Floorspace:	Occupied	411,631m²
		Vacant[1]	69,061m²
		Total	480,692m²
		Total built by the Development corporation included in above	306,207m²
	Number of Firms		232
	Employees: (WTE[2])	Male	5,859.5
		Female	2,771.0
Shopping Floorspace	Town Centre		39,914m²
	Out of Centre		6,778m²
	Neighbourhood Centres		6,021m²
	Corner Shops		890m²
	Total		53,603m²
	Total built by the Development Corporation included in above		10,594m²
Office Floorspace	Occupied		64,843m²
	Vacant		3,485m²
	Total		68,328m²
	Total built by the Development Corporation included in above		35,018m²
Services	Roads:	Principal	9.68 miles
		Non Principal	81.24 miles
	Total		90.92 miles

Notes: [1] Includes not in operation

[2] WTE means whole time equivalent

GLENROTHES DEVELOPMENT CORPORATION
LIST OF BOARD MEMBERS, CHIEF OFFICERS AND HEADS OF DEPARTMENT

1. MEMBERS

Sir Hector McNeill	1948-1952	Mr R S Watt	1971-1981
Mr John Sneddon	1948-1960	Sir George Sharp	1973-1986
Major R L Christie	1948-1953	Mr R King	1975-1988
Dr L T M Gray	1948-1953	Mr J B Kay	1975-1978
Mr J M Mitchell	1948-1952	Mrs M Wood	1976-1984
Bailie D Wright	1948-1954	Mr R W Adams	1976-1984
Lady Ruth Balfour	1948-1960	Mr J R McNally	1976-1980
Mr J Wright	1948-1952	Mr J Stevenson	1978-1980
Mr W C G Peterkin	1952-1955	Mr R K L Gough	1978-1989
Mr A W Mudie	1952-1970	Mr A M Sharp	1979-1984
Sir Garnet Wilson	1952-1960	Mr A Philp	1981-1984
Mr T W Gray	1953-1959	Mr I A McCrone	1981-1996
Mr R N Campbell	1956-1959	Mr W J Turcan	1982-1985
Dr J B Fleming	1958-1969	Mrs A Ferguson	1985-1991
Col A J S Watson	1958-1971	Mrs V Gemmell	1985-1990
Mr A Devlin*	1959-1978	Mr G Hepburn	1985-1989
Mr R R Taylor	1959-1978	Mr D C Mason	1985-1996
Lord Hughes	1960-1964	Mr J A G Fiddes	1986-1996
Mrs D P Verden Anderson	1960-1968	Prof C Blake	1987-1996
Sir J M McWilliam	1962-1970	Mr D B B Smith	1989-1996
Mr A L McLure	1965-1975	Mr J Fitzpatrick	1989-1991
Mr J B Rae	1965-1967	Mr J W MacDougall	1990-1996
Mrs E B Henderson	1968-1975	Mrs F M Havenga	1991-1996
Mr T Hunter Thomson	1969-1976	Mr R J Taylor	1992-1996
Mr D A Shepherd	1970-1976	Mrs J H P Buchanan	1992-1996
Sir David Erskine	1970-1973		

*Mr Devlin was the longest serving New Town Corporation member in the UK.

2. CHIEF OFFICERS AND HEADS OF DEPARTMENT

J M Roger, Secretary & Legal Adviser	1949-1962
F A B Preston, General Manager	1949-1958
E A Ferriby, Chief Architect & Planning Officer	1949-1950
J Young, Chief Finance Officer	1949-1956
H Pollitt, Chief Estates Officer	1949-1959
P Tinto, Chief Architect & Planning Officer	1950-1964
J Dargie, Chief Finance Officer	1957-1974
Brig A R Purches, General Manager	1958-1962
L Higgs, Housing Manager	1959-1964
I Drummond, Landscaping & Forestry Officer	1959-1968
W Rankin, Valuation & Estates Officer	1959-1982
K Ferguson, Secretary & Legal Adviser/Director of Administration & Legal Services	1962-1981
Brig R S Doyle, General Manager/Chief Executive	1962-1976
D H Allan, Housing Officer/Director of Housing	1964-1976
G A Sutherland, Chief Engineer/Director of Engineering	1964-1984
M C Williams, Chief Architect & Planning Officer/ Director of Architecture & Planning	1965-1972
T McIntosh, Landscaping & Forestry Officer	1968-1983
J A F McCombie, Chief Estates Officer/Director of Property Development /Commercial Director/Director of Development	1970-1993
J A F McCombie, General Manager	1993-1996
J L Coghill, Executive Architect/Chief Architect & Planning Officer/ Director of Architecture & Planning	1972-1977
J Tippen, Technical Co-ordination Officer/Depute Commercial Director/Director of Property Services	1973-1992
A F Laird, Chief Finance Officer/Director of Finance	1975-1985
K G Fenwick, Director of Housing	1976-1982
W M Cracknell, Chief Executive	1976-1993
J Baird, Director of Architecture & Planning	1977-1980
A H Bannerman, Director of Architecture & Planning/Technical Director/Director of Development Services	1980-1992
A A Dow, Director of Admin & Legal Services	1980-1990
J A F McFarlane, Director of Housing	1982-1985
T. Callaway, Director of Finance	1986-1987
M C Dyke, Director of Finance/Director of Management Services	1988-1993
J D Elder, Secretary & Legal Adviser/Director of Admin & Legal Services	1990-1996
A Wyles, Director of Technical Services	1992-1996
C R Cramb, Head of Disposals	1992-1995
J Duncan, Director of Finance	1993-1996
J Reade, Head of Valuation Services	1993-1995

Staff Reunion in the Rothes Halls, 2 December 1995

INDEX

INDEX